Health Ques
Your Children Ask

by Cory SerVaas, M.D.

THOMAS NELSON PUBLISHERS
Nashville

Published in Nashville, Tennessee, by Thomas Nelson, Inc., and distributed by Canada by Lawson Falle, Ltd., Cambridge, Ontario.

Printed in the United States of America.

ISBN 0-8407-3033-0

Table of Contents

Children Ask Questions About

Design by JMH Corporation

We thank our many young readers who have
contributed to this book.

We are indebted to Elizabeth Peterson, M.D.
Elizabeth Terry, R.N., C.P.N.P. and to
Jean White, editor; for their assistance
in preparing the manuscript.

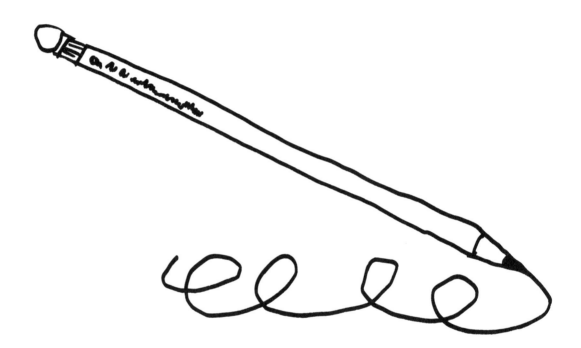

Health Questions Your Children Ask

This book is made up of questions and answers that have appeared in the magazines of The Children's Better Health Institute, magazines that reach millions of young readers.

Child Life, America's oldest children's magazine, first appeared in 1922; *Children's Playmate* in 1929; and *Jack and Jill* in 1938. Newer members of the magazine family are *Children's Digest* (1950), *Humpty Dumpty's* (1952), and *Turtle* (1979).

All of the magazines contain stories, poems, games, and puzzles to stimulate young minds and imaginations. More important, each magazine teaches the fundamentals of health, nutrition, safety and fitness. And each includes the "Ask Dr. Cory" pages where children's questions appear along with my answers.

Yes, real children do write letters and send them to the magazines. Most of these young correspondents are seven to ten years of age. They live in small towns, in cities, and on farms, in all parts of the United States.

They ask all kinds of questions. Some are just for fun. For example: "When someone takes a Tylenol how does it know where you're hurting so it can go to that spot?" "Why don't we feel upside down when the world is?" "Why do puppies have their eyes closed when they are born and people don't?"

Others voice a poignant cry from the heart:

"My Granpa died of lung cancer. My Dad smokes. How can I get him to stop? I don't want to lose him too."

"My Mom and my natural Dad been fighting a long time. Please tell me what to do."

"Why do people have to die when you don't want them to? How does it feel to die?"

All children ask questions about health and illness.

A typical situation is that a near relative is diagnosed as having cancer. The child overhears an adult conversation and asks, "What's cancer?" This is the time for a matter-of-fact answer: Here's how cancer acts on the body. Here's what the doctors do to help the body fight it.

Cory SerVaas, M.D.

v

GOOd EXERCISE

Chapter 1

Children Ask Questions About

Their Bodies

Almost from birth, children are interested in—and curious about—their own bodies. Most babies focus their eyes for the first time on their own hands. We see a wondrous look of delight on the face of the infant who has just discovered his own five fingers waving, at a convenient distance from his eyes. Next, he will discover his even more wonderful toes. What excitement!

Soon after the child begins to talk, he will begin to ask questions. The child will ask "Why is the sky blue?" and then, in the next breath, "Why does John have a penis and Mary doesn't?" and "Why are people's skins different colors?"

Does a parent need to have all the answers on the tip of the tongue? No, but it's well to be prepared for the questions that have to do with such sensitive matters as sex and race. If these questions don't get a prompt, matter-of-fact answer the child may attach too much importance to them.

Otherwise, it's perfectly all right to say "I don't know, but I'll try to find out." Parents don't need to be walking encyclopedias, but they do need to respond when a child asks questions. Otherwise, when the child is older and has a really important question to ask, he may go elsewhere for an answer.

1

Dear Dr cory

Dear Dr. cory:
Is the heart shaped
diffrent then how we
draw it?

Your frien
Heather G.
Balto., Maryland

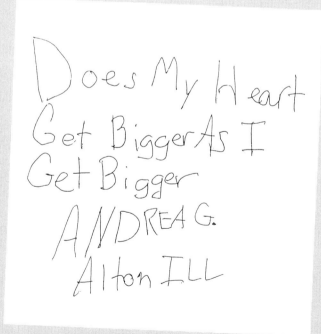

Does My Heart
Get Bigger As I
Get Bigger
ANDREA G.
Alton ILL

Dear Heather:

The human heart doesn't look much like the heart you draw, but it is somewhat the same shape. The heart has two rounded chambers at the top that are somewhat like the "humps" you draw, and it does taper, or grow smaller, at the bottom, though it does not come to a sharp point. It's safe to guess that the person who first drew a red "Valentine's Day" heart knew something about the real heart and how it works.

Dear Andrea:

Your heart is about the size of your clenched fist. As your body grows, your heart grows with it.

Dear: Dr. Cory

How to close does
my heart wark?

By

Heather N.
Phoenix
Arazona

Dear Dr. Cory:
when you are
running and having
fun, why does
your heart beat
faster?
Sandra W.
Fountain Valley,
Claifornia

Dear Heather:

Your heart has four hollow chambers surrounded by walls made of strong muscle tissue. The chambers fill with blood, then the muscles squeeze together and force the blood out into the blood vessels. The blood flows throughout your body, bringing it the oxygen and nutrients it needs, and removing waste products.

The heart beats because of a very special type of nerve fiber and tissue in the upper part of the heart. This is called the pacemaker of the heart. It sends out electrical impulses or signals to the rest of the heart. These signals are continuous, day and night. They cause the heart to contract in a sequence that allows the chambers to fill and empty and refill in a regular, coordinated cycle, making circulation of blood to the whole body possible.

Dear Sandra:

The body's blood goes where it is most needed at any point in time. When you are running or doing any kind of increased physical activity, your bones, muscles, heart, and lungs need more blood than do other areas of the body. The heart pumps faster to meet the demands of these body parts during activity. This is why your pulse and heartbeat are faster during or just after activity.

The blood supply to the brain, however, is always the same, no matter what the rest of the body is doing. That way the brain always has an adequate supply of blood to provide energy.

3

. . . About Their Bodies

Why is my blood red and my veins blue,

January P.
Trimont, MN,

Dear January:

Your blood is red. Blood coming from the heart and lungs is bright cherry red, and it is carried by the arteries. Blood that has delivered its oxygen to the tissues and is returning to the heart and lungs to be recharged is a deep maroon red. The veins that carry this returning blood are in some places very close to the surface of the skin. When you see this dark blood through your skin and through the walls of the vein it looks blue.

Dear Dr. Cory,
When I went to the Doctor the nurse wrapped a black band around my arm and then pumpud it up. what does that tell the doctor?
Billy F,
LouisVille,
Kentucky

4

Dear Billy:

The nurse was using a blood pressure cuff around your arm. Taking your blood pressure tells how hard your blood is pushing against the sides of your arteries. When one of the chambers of the heart, the left ventricle, squeezes itself together, it forces blood out into the arteries. The major arteries have to expand to receive the blood, and this causes pressure. The muscular lining of the arteries resists some of this pressure, so the blood is then pushed on into the smaller blood vessels of the body. The pressure is important. If the arteries don't have enough pressure from the blood pushing against their inside walls, then the blood can't go into the smaller vessels and it can't get uphill to the head. But if there is too much pressure, the blood presses too hard against the artery walls, sometimes causing one of them to break. This usually becomes more of a problem as a person grows older. But it is a good idea to have your blood pressure checked routinely, because some children do have high blood pressure.

Dear Dr. Cory:
How many times does your heart beat every hour. How many times does your heart beat every minute or second?

Noell H.
Frett
Tualatin, Oregon

Dear Dr. Cory:

Sometimes when I yawn, my ears pop. Why is that?

Edward Brewer
Ilion, N.Y.

Dear Noell:

A newborn baby girl's heart beats around 140 times per minute, while a newborn boy's heart usually beats a little more slowly, around 125 beats per minute. By the time they are about six months old both boys' and girls' hearts will beat around 100 beats per minute. The heart gradually slows down as the child grows, and a grownup's heart beats about 70 times per minute. That's a little more than once per second, and about 420 times per hour.

The heart beats faster when you exercise, and more slowly when you sleep.

Dear Edward:

The *eustachian tube* is a tube that connects the inside of your ear to your throat. The opening of the tube to the throat is closed except when you are swallowing, yawning, and sneezing. The outside and the inside of the ear are divided by a thin membrane called the eardrum, or the *tympanic membrane*. The eustachian tube helps to equalize pressure on either side of the eardrum. When the opening of the eustachian tube to the throat is opened during a yawn, sneeze, or a swallow, the pressure inside the ear changes a little. This causes the popping sensation that you feel.

5

> Dear Dr. Cory:
> Can earrings hurt the ears in anyway?
>
> Christy M.
> Miami, Indiana

> Dear Doctor Cory;
>
> Why do we have earwax?
>
> Susan B.
> Hudsonville Michigan

Dear Christy:

Too tight earrings can really hurt, but most of the time earrings are harmless. For those of us who are allergic to some of the metals used in earrings, the metal may cause an unpleasant rash.

Piercing the ears may cause problems. The openings may become infected, or they may heal closed. Some people create thick bumpy scars called keloids. When these people have their ears pierced, a large and unsightly scar may result. Attempts to remove the scar may result in a larger scar, so be cautious about having your ears pierced if you belong to a family that forms keloids.

If you have pierced ears, keep the earring posts clean. If your ears tend to become infected, you may dip the posts in an antibiotic ointment such as Neosporin before inserting the posts.

Another word of caution: Pierced-ear earrings that are dangling or hooped should *not* be worn during play or active sports, as an earring may be caught on something and result in a painfully torn ear lobe.

Dear Susan:

The earwax, or cerumen, is produced by a type of sweat gland in the ear. The sticky, pasty earwax, along with a few hairs, helps to protect the ear from outside particles that might enter and damage it. Sometimes the earwax is quite thick and builds up. It then needs to be removed by a doctor or a nurse because it can interfere with hearing. You shouldn't try to remove it, because you could severely damage your ear by poking objects into it. If done incorrectly this procedure can also push the wax in deeper. However, sometimes the doctor might recommend special ear drops to be used regularly to keep the wax from being excessive.

Overall, earwax is one of our body's protective devices and should be left alone.

Dear Dr. Cory
When you spin around in circles why
when you stop it looks like the world
is turning?
Sarah R.
Hoisington, Kansas

Dear Sarah:

The reason it seems like the world is turning after you stop spinning is to be found in the inner ear. The inner ear is made up of semicircular canals. These canals are filled with fluid that controls balance. The fluid is moving from the spin and doesn't stop immediately when you stop spinning, thus giving the sensation of continuing movement of things around you.

Dear Dr cory,
What happens
when you yawn?
Gloria M.
Marlboro, NY.

Dear Gloria:

A yawn is a wide opening of the throat so you can take a deep, slow breath. We usually yawn when we are tired and sleepy and when we've been taking only small, shallow breaths. Waste gasses have been piling up in our lungs, and this triggers a yawn that releases the waste gasses and brings in a supply of new air. Yawning is your body's way of telling you that you should either go to bed and to sleep, or get up and walk around in the fresh air.

7

Dear Dr. Cory,
Is all watching T.V. when
the T.V. is all scratchy and fuzzy
stuff ok for your eyes? Someone told me it
would make you blind. Will it?
Amy F.
Westminster, Maryland

Dear Amy:

Watching TV that is scratchy and fuzzy is not healthy for your eyes. Since the brain does not like fuzzy pictures, the eye does its best to correct the fuzzy image. Prolonged watching of a fuzzy picture makes the eye work very hard, and can cause eyestrain and headaches. This does not create blindness but it definitely is not good for your eyes.

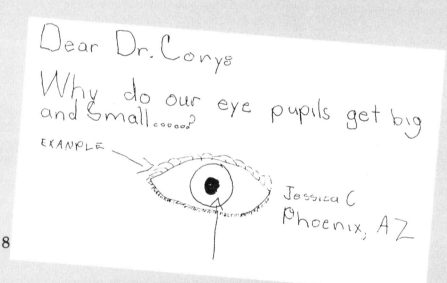

Dear Dr. Cory,
Why do our eye pupils get big
and small.......?
EXANPLE
Jessica C
Phoenix, AZ

Dear Dr. Cory:
How many bone
we have?
Stephan
Hampton

8

Dear Jessica:

Your eye is like a camera. The black center part that we call the pupil is an opening that admits light to the retina at the back of the eye. It is like the lens that lets light reach the film in the back of a camera.

The opening gets larger or smaller to control the amount of light that enters the eye. When the light is bright, as in the middle of the day, the pupil is small. When the light is dim, the pupil gets larger.

We have all noticed how we are temporarily blinded when we walk out of a dark movie theater onto a sunlit street. That's because it takes a little time for our pupils to adjust to the bright light.

Dear Dr Cory,
When I am about 21 years, will
my bones stay just ~~about~~ as they
are for the rest of my life?

Sherry S.
Kansas City, Kansas

Dear Sherry:

It's true that a person's bones are fully formed by the time he or she is 21 years old. But, like other parts of the body, bones are constantly changing on the inside. Many choices you make—like the foods you eat, regular exercise, and choosing not to smoke—really do make a difference in how strong and healthy your bones are, no matter whether you're a kid, or a grownup.

Dear Droctor Cory,
Why do your baby teeth fall out?
and your permanent teeth do not fall out?

April N.
Mahnomen, Minn.

Dear April:

When you were born, you didn't have any teeth. As you grew, a set of baby teeth developed that were the right size for your mouth when you were only a few years old. Now that you are getting older and you are growing, your baby teeth are not large enough. They will fall out, one at a time, and you will grow a new tooth in place of each baby tooth. This new set of teeth will be your permanent teeth for the rest of your life. Be sure to brush your teeth after every meal, and visit your dentist twice a year so that your new set of teeth will stay strong and healthy.

Dear Stephanie:

A baby is usually born with 270 bones in his skeletal framework. However, because some bones grow together or fuse, by the time a person becomes an adult he or she has just 206 bones.

Your arms and hands contain the most bones—sixty-four in all—and there are sixty-two in your feet and legs. Your ribs count twenty-four and your spinal column has twenty-six bones.

9

Dear Dr. Cory:
If everything else stops growing when we get older, why do our hair and nails keep growing?

James S.
Boise, Idaho

Dear Jamie:

Our hair and nails are, in a way, extensions of our skin. Although it is not noticeable, our skin continues to grow and replace itself, even when the body has stopped growing taller. Some skin cells die and flake off; new skin cells grow to replace them. In the same way, new hair and nail cells are constantly growing to replace old cells that die, and this makes the hair and nails longer.

In reality, the entire body is constantly replacing old cells with new ones, so good nutrition is important at all phases of life, not just during the childhood "growth" years.

Dear Dr. Cory:
Why do we have belly buttons?

Leslie M.
Harrington, Wa.

Dear Leslie:

Belly buttons, sometimes called navels or umbilici, are located in the center of our abdomens. We all have them. A belly button marks the spot where the umbilical cord was attached to the unborn baby. The umbilical cord has two arteries containing blood that carries nourishment and oxygen from the mother to the baby and one vein carrying waste and carbon dioxide from the baby to the mother. When the baby is born, the umbilical cord is no longer needed. The cord is cut by the person who delivers the baby; this is not painful for the mother or the baby. The small part of the cord that was attached to the baby dries up and falls off. Your belly button is nothing more than a little scar that shows where you were attached to your mother.

Dear Docter Cory:
How do people cry?

Jamie J.
Osmond, Nebraska

Dear Jamie:

Every time your eyelid closes you are crying. There are tear ducts located on the inner corners of each eye. When you blink, suction is created and pulls some fluid out through the tear ducts. The fluid is what we call tears. The tear glands, which supply the tear ducts, are located over the outer corner of each eye. The fluid, or tears, helps to wash irritating and harmful substances out of the eye and to keep the eye from becoming too dry.

When you cry, the tear glands make more tears than the tear duct can drain, and the tears "spill over."

Dear Dr. Cory:
Some one told me that reading in the dark is bad for your eyes. How can it harm them? Also, my friends told me that if I tried on someone's glasses, I would go blind. Is that true?

Toi G.
Portland, Oregon

11

Dear Toi:

Reading in dim light does injure your eyes. Ideally, an adequate light should come from over your shoulder when you're reading. Reading in too bright light, however, may also be harmful. Don't read with the sun shining directly on your paper. The sun's rays are reflected from the paper into your eyes. The lenses of your eyes focus this energy on a very small area, which may be injured by intense light. Also, never look directly at the sun. This might burn the retina of your eye and permanently injure it. The result is a blind spot right in the middle of your visual field. When this happens, a person can see all around an object he or she is looking at but cannot see the object itself.

Trying on someone else's glasses will not cause blindness. It is not a good idea, however, to wear glasses that belong to someone else. Glasses are prescribed by a doctor and made especially for the owner and no one else. If you think that you may need glasses, talk to your parents or school nurse about having your eyes examined.

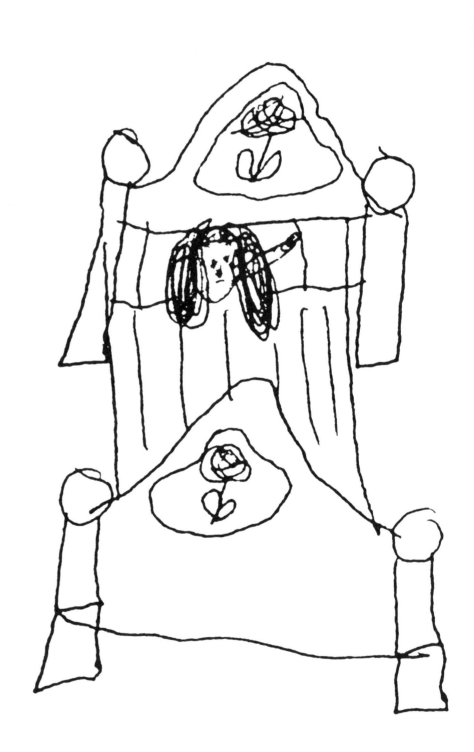

Chapter 2

Children Ask Questions About

Their Illnesses

Chickenpox (or, sometimes, chicken *pops*) is the subject of many letters to The Children's Better Health Institute. The reason may be that since we have had no dependable vaccine against chickenpox, it is likely to be the only one of the old-fashioned "children's diseases" that today's boys and girls experience.

Chickenpox may be the first disease that makes the child really uncomfortable, with fever, malaise, and itchy rash. It may be the child's first experience with being sick enough to stay in bed. This makes a lasting impression, and children tend to remember "when I had chickenpox" after many other childhood experiences are forgotten.

Earache, dental caries, colds, flu, and tonsillitis are among the other health problems about which children ask questions. Many are "why" questions, and these present an excellent opportunity for teaching basic hygiene. Tell your child how good handwashing habits, regular toothbrushing, good diet and exercise can help to prevent a recurrence of the health problems he experiences.

Dear Docter Cory:
What are hiccups?
And why don't they stop?

Courtney J.
Bend, Oregon

Dear Courtney:

An upset stomach, nervousness, even certain diseases may cause hiccups. There is a thin sheet of muscle, called the *diaphragm*, that separates your stomach from other organs. The diaphragm contracts and relaxes to help you breathe. Sometimes it will start "jumping" or having spasms, and that's what makes you hiccup.

You can sometimes stop hiccups by breathing deeply or holding your breath for a while. Some people can stop their hiccups by breathing into a paper bag. But, for most people, hiccups last for just a few minutes and then stop without help.

14

Hiccup!

Dear Docter Cory:
Some times when
I'm laying in bed I
hear a beep noise in my
ear. Why do I get that? What
is that cald?

Jennifer D.
Londonderry N.H.

Dear Dr. Cory,

How do you get headaches?
What do they do?

Your friend,
Shannon S
Waukesha, WI

Dear Shannon:

Like other kinds of pain, headaches are usually a signal that something is wrong in your body. For example, a headache may be one of the first signs of flu or some other infection. A headache may signal that you are mistreating your eyes by reading in a poor light or watching TV for too long. A headache may signal that you've eaten food that doesn't agree with you—for example, some people who are allergic to chocolate get a headache from eating even a small piece of chocolate candy. You may get a headache from breathing stuffy indoor air.

Adults' headaches are often due to tension brought on by stress or worry.

Some headaches will go away if you take light exercise in the fresh air, so try taking a walk. If that doesn't work, lie down in a dark room and try to take a nap; your headache will probably be gone when you wake up.

Tell an adult when you have a headache. One headache once in a while is nothing to worry about, but if you have headaches often, or if they are severe, you should see a doctor.

Dear Jennifer:

The condition of hearing sounds in the ear when there are no sounds that other people hear is called tinnitus, and it is quite common. It is usually caused by a buildup of wax in the ear, and when the wax is removed the sounds will stop.

Some people hear a hissing or buzzing sound, others hear a ringing or, as in your case, a beeping.

There are many things that can cause tinnitus, and some of them are more serious. For example, in an older person tinnitus may signal high blood pressure and the possibility of a stroke. So, if you keep hearing noises that aren't there, you should have your ears checked by a doctor. In the meantime, if the beeping is keeping you awake, try playing soft music on a radio when you are in bed.

15

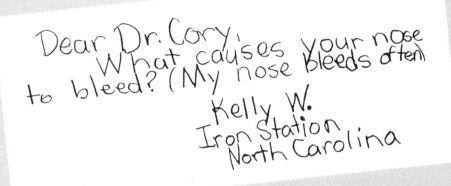

Dear Dr. Cory,
What causes your nose to bleed? (My nose bleeds often)
Kelly W.
Iron Station
North Carolina

Dear Kelly:

Nosebleeds are common during childhood, but decrease in the teenage years. Most start in the front part of the nose when a small blood vessel is broken. Nosebleeds are often caused by nasal irritation from colds, dry air (particularly in winter), and nose picking. Sometimes the use of a room humidifier, or applying a little vaseline twice a day to the center wall just inside the nose, will help to relieve the dryness and irritation. Avoid aspirin, because it can increase the tendency of the body to bleed and can make nosebleeds last longer. Some other causes of nosebleeds include tumors, blood diseases, direct injury to the nose, severe high blood pressure, and objects pushed up into the nose.

Contact your doctor if you have frequent nosebleeds, ones in which you lose a lot of blood, or if you can't tell where the bleeding is starting.

To treat a nosebleed, follow this procedure:

1. Blow the nose once.
2. Cover the nose with a clean cloth or tissue.
3. Using the thumb and forefinger, firmly pinch the *lower* part of the nose, so that the nostrils are closed.
4. Tilt the head *slightly forward*.
5. Pinch continually for five minutes by the clock.
6. Remove the cloth. Do not blow or pick the nose.
7. If bleeding begins again, repeat the sequence.

16

Dear, Dr. Cory

<u>Why</u> do we need
our temperature taken?
  Pam R.
  Rockford, Illinois

Dear Pam:

The thermometer your doctor (or the nurse, or your mother) uses to take your temperature gives important information about what is going on inside your body. The normal temperature of your body is 98.6 F. If your temperature goes much higher, it is usually because your body is fighting some kind of infection. A high body temperature means fever, and fever always means that something has gone wrong inside the body.

Dear Dr. Cory,
Where do
sneezes come
from and how
many sneezes
can a person
make?
  Shayna M.
  San Bernardino

Dear Shayna:

Sneezes are triggered by the irritation of the mucous membranes lining the nose. The cause of the irritation may be a bit of dust, plant pollen, or pepper that has gotten into the nose. Pepper is an irritant that will cause almost everyone to sneeze. Sneezing is a way of getting rid of the irritant, whatever it is, and sneezing will usually continue until it is gone.

The sneeze is a reflex act causing you to take a deep breath and then let it out explosively through the nose and mouth. Two or three sneezes will usually clear the nose of whatever was causing the problem.

17

Dear Rebecca:

You should tell your parents any time you have an earache. The pain you feel from an earache may be an important warning sign. It usually indicates that you have an ear infection.

The most common type of ear infection is called a middle ear infection. These may be caused by bacteria or, sometimes, by a virus. Many people get them when they have a cold. When you get a cold a small tube called the eustachian tube that leads from the ear to the throat can become blocked. This keeps bacteria from draining into the throat and traps it in the ear. When this fluid gets trapped it may become infected and put pressure on the eardrum. The eardrum may turn red (the doctor will see this when he examines you) and you may begin to feel the pain of an earache.

If this is not treated, the infection can spread. Also, repeated untreated infections may damage the middle ear bones and cause diminished hearing.

Other causes of earaches also exist. When the eustachian tube that connects the middle ear to the throat becomes blocked, air pressure can build up and cause pain. Fluid may push on the eardrum and be uncomfortable as well as cause decreased hearing. Pimples in the ear canal and swimmer's ear are also painful. Even impacted cerumen (ear wax) can cause pain.

18

Dear Amy:

Seasickness results from irritation of the balance organs in your ears. Excessive motion a person is not accustomed to may cause it. Irritation by drugs, illness, or head injury may also cause the nausea of seasickness.

Seasickness gets its name from travel by ship on the ocean, but you can also get motion sickness from traveling in a car or airplane. If this happens to you often, ask your doctor for medicine you can take before traveling, to prevent motion sickness.

Dear Dr. Cory,
I had my adenoids taken out when I was 5 years old. What in the heck do adenoids do?
Heather R
Atlanta, Georgia

Dear Dr. Cory:
Why do you have tonsils? Because I keep having trouble with mine.
Jennifer W
Downingtown, Pennsylvania

Dear Jennifer and Heather:

Tonsils and adenoids are pairs of small organs in your throat area that help filter the air you breathe so that you don't breathe germs into your lungs. The tonsils are in the very back of your throat, on each side, behind your back teeth. Adenoids are located above the tonsils, behind the nose and sinus area. Both of these tissues vary in size from person to person, and often become smaller with age.

Unfortunately, these two tissues can swell, for a variety of reasons, and create a problem. The adenoids when swollen can make it difficult to breathe through the nose, and may hinder sinus and palate development. Adenoids become larger due to allergy, sinus problems, or infection. When the tonsils are enlarged they can create problems with swallowing, speech, or sore throats. Infection, sinus drainage, or allergy, play a part in tonsillar swelling.

The most common reason for removal of the tonsils is recurring or chronic infection. The incidence of throat infections usually peaks in early school age and declines in the teen years through adulthood. To decide if the tonsils need to be removed, the doctor will carefully assess the frequency and severity of throat infections, the incidence of bacterial infections (strep), and the size of the tonsils.

Most doctors do not advise tonsillectomy unless the tonsils have had at least three infections in each of three years, or six infections in any one year.

Removing the adenoids frequently accompanies tonsillectomy, or the adenoids alone may be removed if the adenoid swelling is chronic and seems to be causing ear infections or fluid, or poor palate growth.

19

Dear Dr. Cory,
What is a viral infection?

Angie P.
Hudson, Wisconsin

Dear Angie:

Viruses are very small living particles that cause many diseases, such as influenza, chickenpox, sore throats, and measles. They are more difficult to deal with than bacterial infections because they cannot be cured by antibiotic medication. Most viral infections eventually go away on their own with a lot of rest, liquids, and care. Sometimes medication for fever, aches, and congestion is helpful. However, never take any medicine without first checking with your parents.

Many viruses are easily passed on from one person to another through the air by sneezing and coughing. Or they can be picked up by touching hands or items, such as toys, that a person with a virus recently handled. That is why it is always helpful in preventing the spread of a virus to practice good hygiene. Frequent handwashing, covering the mouth and nose when sneezing or coughing, and keeping personal items such as glasses and eating utensils separate from those used by others, are important.

Dear Dr. Cory:
WHY DO kids
Have TO Have
SHOTS?

Melissa D
Terra Bella,
California

Dear Melissa:

Different kinds of shots are given for different reasons. Your immunizations contain small amounts of killed germs, which your body responds to by making antibodies. These antibodies then attack that kind of germ whenever they come across it. This prevents your getting the kind of disease carried by that germ.

Antibiotic shots are used to fight infections. They contain chemicals that kill the germs that cause infection.

20

Dear Amber:

Scarlet fever is a disease caused by a bacteria or germ called streptococcus, or strep. Strep infections cause fever and a very sore throat. Sometimes it causes a special red rash, and then the term scarlet fever is used. This rash is very red, and feels rough (like sandpaper!) and is found under the arms, the groin, and the trunk. You can only catch it from someone who has a strep infection, by touching that person or by breathing the same air near that person.

Scarlet fever can only be prevented by staying away from someone who has it and not sharing toys or food dishes when the person is sick.

The good news is that since strep is a bacteria, it is killed by antibiotics. A visit to the doctor, plus a throat culture, will help to keep strep in its place.

Dear Erin:

The common cold is not just one disease. There are about 400 different viruses that cause cold or flu-like symptoms. Vaccines could be made for each of these viruses, but it would be very expensive and most people would object to having 400 cold or flu shots every year or two!

Unfortunately, we do not have a safe, effective antiviral drug. Penicillin and antibiotics work only on bacteria—not on viruses.

Dear Doctor Cory,
Can people catch
Colds from animals?
From
Cory

Dear Cory:

You've asked an interesting question. No, people don't catch colds or flu from animals, because these are viral infections, and the viruses that cause infections in humans are different from those that cause infections in animals.

There are, however, bacterial diseases that can be passed from pets to their owners. In most cases the germs are in the animals' wastes (feces and urine). This is why dogs should not be allowed to relieve themselves on grass where children play. It is why sandboxes should be covered, so cats cannot use them for litterboxes. It is why you should always wash your hands very carefully after cleaning a pet's cage or tank.

Almost any kind of animal can carry salmonella, which is an intestinal infection. Turtles often have it, and if you let a turtle walk around on the kitchen cabinet or drainboard while you are cleaning the turtle tank, the germs left behind by the turtle can get into salad greens or other food that is eaten uncooked, and infect the whole family.

Cats carry toxoplasmosis, which is usually a mild disease but dangerous for a pregnant woman as it can cause birth defects in her unborn child. Cats and dogs may carry visceral larva migrans, a worm parasite that can infect humans. Birds, hamsters, gerbils, guinea pigs and even fish have diseases that can infect humans.

This does not mean that pets are dangerous, or that you should not be allowed to have pets. It just means you should wash your hands carefully after touching pets and before you touch food that you or other humans may eat.

Dear Dr. Cory,
Do you catch a cold because you've been in cold weather?
Ben S.

Dear Dr. Cory:
How do you'r noses get so runny. And how do you get colds
Darcy W.
Deltona, Florida

Dear Ben:

That's a very good question! People do seem to have many more colds when the weather turns cold. But the reason is *not* because we are outside in the cold weather. In the winter we spend more time indoors, and it's there that the germs that cause colds are passed from one person to another.

Dear Darcy:

The runny nose is a normal part of having a cold. The virus infection settles in the mucous membrane that lines your nose, causing a watery discharge that carries pus and mucus—and virus particles—with it. The runny nose is a part of your body's way of getting rid of what is making you sick.

You "catch" a cold when you take into your body virus particles from the body of someone else who has a cold.

Because virus particles are in the discharge from your nose, keep it away from other people. Use disposable tissues to blow your nose, and place the used tissues in a closed paper bag so no one else will touch them.

Does your nose run in the summer when you don't have a cold? If it does, you may suffer from an allergy. Many people are allergic to plant pollens that float in the air in summer. This used to be called hay fever, though it usually has nothing to do with hay. It probably got that name because many weeds and trees produce pollen at about the same time farmers are making hay.

23

Dear Dr. Cory
what Are Measles?
Stephanie B
Millville N.J.

Dear Doctor Cory,
what are the German Measles

Allyson
O'Fallon Mo.

Dear Stephanie:

Thanks to modern medicine and the development of immunizations against many diseases such as measles, people no longer get the measles as often as they used to. Unfortunately some teenagers and college students still come down with measles because they were not immunized when they were kids.

Measles is caused by a virus. This virus is very easily spread from one person to another through direct contact with the infected person's nasal or throat fluids. Unlike bacterial infections, viral infections cannot be treated with an antibiotic; there are no medicines to cure them.

Dear Allyson:

German measles (or rubella) is an illness caused by a virus. This means that medicines such as antibiotics are not helpful in treating the disease. It is a very contagious illness passed by the person who has the disease to other people by nose or mouth secretions, blood, feces, or urine. A person is contagious with the virus from seven days before the rash appears until seven or eight days after the rash has gone.

German measles is often hard to diagnose because other viruses produce similar rashes. The rash begins on the face and then spreads quickly to the rest of the body. By the second day it has a fine, red, pinpoint appearance. It is mildly itchy and usually clears by the third day. If there is fever, it seldom is higher than 101 degrees F. The lymph nodes toward the back of the neck are often enlarged and tender. Once a person has

had German measles he will be protected from getting it again by the natural immunity created by the disease.

Currently, most people are vaccinated against German measles (rubella) when they get their measles, mumps, rubella (MMR) vaccination at 15 months of age. Now most cases of German measles occur in teenagers and adults who were not vaccinated when they were younger. The virus is of particular concern because of its danger to an unborn child. A fetus whose mother gets the disease early in pregnancy can be born with severe defects, including blindness, deafness, and heart defects. So it is very important for all persons to be vaccinated, not only to protect themselves from the disease, but to protect nonimmune pregnant women from the disease.

24

The symptoms of measles—such as fever, slight cough, and coldlike symptoms—can be treated with acetaminophen (such as Tylenol), rest, and plenty of fluids. Within two or three days a rash appears, the temperature rises, and the person can seem very ill. Usually within a day or two the person feels much better. However, there can be very serious complications, such as pneumonia and encephalitis (swelling of the brain). For these reasons, it is important for all children to be vaccinated against measles.

Once a person has had measles he won't get them again.

Dear Dr Cory,
I want to ask you how many times do people have chicken pox or do all people have chicken pox one time. My mother said that all people have one time is that true?

Your friend,
Nora K.

Dear Dr. Cory
How do we know when we have chicken pops and why can't we go outside when we have chiken pops.
Your friend,
Adriana T.

Dear Adriana and Nora:

A very contagious illness caused by a virus, chickenpox usually begins with a slight fever. Then the person breaks out in a rash that looks like little blisters. Soothing treatments such as cool baths help to relieve the itching, or the doctor may prescribe medication. Aspirin should *not* be given to children who have chickenpox or flu; acetaminophen is recommended if a fever or pain medicine is needed. Most people get over this disease in one or two weeks.

When you have chickenpox your body makes and stores up substances called antibodies that will kill the chickenpox virus, and these should protect you from this disease the rest of your life. So most people have chickenpox just once. It is possible, however, that some babies or small children who have a very light case may not be able to build up this immunity from their first attack of chickenpox, so they might be infected a second time, but this rarely happens.

One good reason for staying indoors when you have chickenpox is to avoid passing the infection to other children. Another is that getting overheated, chilled, or over-tired could lead to complications, while staying indoors and resting quietly will help you to get well as soon as possible.

25

Dear Dr. Cory:
Why do you get the mumps and how can you tell that you have them.

KATIE W.
DEERBROOK, WISCONSIN

Dear Katie:

Mumps is a contagious disease caused by a virus. It is spread by direct contact with a person who has the disease. The virus is present in the saliva and the secretions of the nose. It causes a painful swelling of the salivary glands. Usually the parotid glands, located just below and in front of the ears, are the main ones affected.

The illness usually begins with fever, muscle pain in the neck, headache, and an overall feeling of illness. Mumps is a much more serious disease for adults. Babies are temporarily protected from the disease through their mother's immunity. When a child becomes fifteen months old, a safe vaccine can be given to protect against mumps. Once a person has had mumps, he or she probably will not get it again. Most cases of mumps are seen in the winter and spring, but mumps can infect a person any time of the year.

One test, to see if you have the mumps, is to try to eat a pickle. When you eat an acid food like a pickle the glands in your mouth produce saliva, and if you have mumps this will be very painful because the glands are infected.

Dear Dr. Cory,
Please tell me what a fungus is. My mother said I might have one on my foot.

Jessica F.
Des Moines, Iowa

Dear Jessica:

Your mother is probably referring to the kind of fungus called athlete's foot. It has that name because many people get it around shower rooms and public swimming pools.

Fungi are plantlike living things that cannot manufacture their own food from the soil as green plants do. Most fungi live on dead plants but a few, like the athlete's foot fungus, can live as parasites on living creatures. They like warm moist conditions such as are found on your feet if your shoes make your feet hot and sweaty.

Athlete's foot causes itching and a dry scaling and thickening of the skin between the toes and on the soles of the feet.

26

Dear Docter Cory,
What is stripe throat

Rachel H.
Edmond. ok

There are antifungal over-the-counter medications which are good for mild cases of athlete's foot. It will help to keep your feet clean and dry. Wear white cotton socks and change them often during the day, or wear sandals that let air get to your feet. To keep from getting athlete's foot, wear rubber sandals around community swimming pools or shower rooms.

There are many different kinds of fungi, including molds, yeast, bacteria, and mushrooms. The "miracle drug" penicillin comes from a fungus mold, and we could not make bread without yeast. Many fungi are useful to man, but some cause serious diseases.

Dear Rachel:

Strep throat is caused by a specific type of bacteria known as beta-hemalytic streptococcus. It is spread by coughing or by direct contact with a person who has strep throat. Try to avoid any contact with a person who has strep throat unless that person has been on an antibiotic for at least 24 hours. The bacteria infect the throat and can cause sore throat and fever, and occasionally headache and upset stomach.

Since strep throat is a bacterial infection it should be treated with antibiotics. It is *very* important to take the prescribed medication for 10 days, because untreated or improperly treated strep throat may lead to rheumatic fever.

Most sore throats are viral infections rather than strep. Your doctor can judge the difference, often with a culture to determine the presence or absence of strep bacteria.

Any combination of sore throat and fever should be taken seriously.

27

Chapter **3**

Children Ask Questions About

Adult Health Problems

A generation or two ago, children saw much more of serious illness and death than they do today. What has made the difference? Today's families are scattered, and grandparents often live far away. People who have more than a very minor illness are usually hospitalized, rather than being cared for at home.

Also, many of today's parents feel their children should be sheltered from the more unpleasant parts of life, and they shrink from discussing serious health problems or death. "Time enough for that later," they say, though this may be because they themselves are uncomfortable talking about such things.

As a result, children learn about adults' health problems chiefly through TV, from the bits of adult conversation they overhear, or from other children equally misinformed. What they piece together from these sources may be much more frightening than a real contact with the problem—for example, a visit to a relative who is recovering from a stroke, or to a neighbor undergoing cancer treatment.

Children deserve matter-of-fact information about cancer, heart attacks, strokes, and diabetes. Tell them how doctors treat these illnesses, and that usually the victim gets better. The child will find the truth less frightening than the pictures his imagination paints.

Dear Dr Cory
   I would like to know
what causes
blindnes?
      Heidi A.
      MTShastaCA

Dear Heidi:

There are many different causes of blindness. An accident such as being hit in the eye with a stone or sharp object can cause blindness. Also, an injury to the nerves or blood vessels that serve the eye can cause blindness. A major cause of blindness among both adults and children is the disease diabetes. Older people may lose most or all of their sight because of glaucoma. Early treatment of diabetes and glaucoma can help prevent blindness from these causes, so it is important to take good care of your eyes and have them checked regularly by a doctor.

Dear Nikki:

Your stomach makes a fluid which helps it digest the food you eat. This fluid is a mild acid, and if there is too much fluid present in your stomach it can destroy the lining and wall of your stomach or intestine. This is probably what happened to your uncle. The part of the stomach wall that was damaged by too much stomach acid is called an ulcer.

An ulcer can be very painful. Some people call this kind of pain heartburn. There are medications that people who have an ulcer can take to heal the ulcer by lowering the amount of stomach acid in the stomach. Sometimes the damage is severe enough to cause bleeding but this kind of ulcer can also be treated by medicine or, in some cases, surgery.

30

Dear Dr. Cory,
   Why do some people get ulcers
or bleeding ulcers?
P.S. My uncle got one. that's why I
asked.
         Nikki S.
         Bidwell, Ohio

Dear Dr. Cory

Why do men and women have to get a blood test before they get married. what does a blood test have to do with getting married does everybody get a blood test that is getting married.

Courtney L
Canoga Park, California

Dear Courtney:

The tests you mention are screening tests that give information only, so the people getting married will know if they have certain diseases. These are diseases that can be passed through intimate contact between husband and wife, or to an unborn child. Having the tests before marriage allows an infected person to get treatment so the disease won't be spread to the spouse, or to a child.

In some states only the woman is tested to see if she is immune to rubella (German measles), because if she had the disease later, while pregnant, her child could be born with serious physical problems. If this is a danger, she can be immunized at the time she marries or before becoming pregnant.

Dear Dr. Cory:
How do you get arthritis?
Anna H.
Orange Park, Florida

Dear Anna:

There are many causes of arthritis, and any joint—places where bones are connected—can be affected. Aging, infections of joints due to an injury, rheumatic fever, and tumors can all bring about arthritis.

Rheumatoid arthritis affects both young and older people and almost three percent of the people in the United States have it. These people feel pain when they move the joint affected by arthritis, and these joints do not move easily and are often swollen.

Arthritis is not contagious. Doctors are working hard to find ways of treating people with the disease. Drugs can ease the pain, and sometimes affected joints can be replaced with new, plastic ones that make it easier and less painful to move.

31

Dear Dr. Cory,
    Why do you get wrinkels when your older?
        Robin Cook
        Dayton, Ohio

Dear Robin:

There are several causes of wrinkles. First of all, the glands that supply oil to the skin are much less active as you get older. Changes in the body's hormones, such as the reduced production of estrogen, can also make the skin less tight. The thin layer of fat that underlies the skin to give it a smooth contour gradually disappears with aging. This sort of "deflates" the skin and makes little folds and wrinkles appear. The single most important cause of wrinkling, however, is the sun. Damage from the sun builds up over the years. It destroys the skin's flexibility and its ability to recover from damage.

Cigarettes are another big cause of wrinkling. Smoking destroys the functioning power of tiny capillaries that carry blood to the inner layers of the skin. Without food from the blood, the skin can't remain healthy.

Dear Heather:

Glaucoma is a buildup of pressure inside the eye, where fluid forms faster than it can drain away through the tiny canals intended for that purpose. This condition is painless, but if it goes on too long it can damage the eye and cause blindness. Doctors check for this condition when they examine the eyes of adults like your grandfather. If discovered in time it can be treated successfully and the person's sight saved.

Dear Dr. Cory,
    I would please like to know what Nocoma is; because my grandpa come to visit and he has it, but nobody will tell me.
    Thank You
        Heather A.
        Virginia Beach, V.A.

Dear Doctor Cory,

Why do people lose their teeth?

Elizabeth G.
Oshkosh, Wisconsin

Dear Elizabeth:

The chief reason adults lose their permanent teeth and have to have dentures is gum disease. Your gums are the skinlike tissue around the base of your teeth.

When this tissue becomes infected it shrinks back from the teeth, so that the roots of the teeth are exposed, and eventually the teeth loosen and fall out. The most common kind of gum disease is called gingivitis.

The first sign of gum disease is usually bleeding when you brush your teeth (though brushing too hard with a too-stiff toothbrush can also cause the gums to bleed or it may be due to a lack of Vitamin C in the diet). If your gums bleed every time you brush, see your dentist and tell him or her.

Gingivitis is usually caused by not brushing the teeth. If the teeth are not brushed regularly, a substance called plaque develops. It sticks to the teeth near the gumline, causing irritation. Cavities and gingivitis may result, if the plaque is not removed. Regular and careful brushing and flossing help to prevent or remove plaque, and to prevent gum disease and tooth loss.

33

DEAR DR. CORY:

What started the aids virus?

Renee R
Union Furnace, Ohio

Dear Renee:

You have asked a question that scientists cannot answer at this time. We think that the AIDS virus may be the result of a change or mutation that happened to some other virus. We believe that the disease AIDS first appeared around 1977, probably in Africa.

Research scientists are like detectives, and the origin of AIDS represents a mystery they haven't yet solved, though they have some clues and some theories.

Dear Dr. Cory:
What are the symptoms of the AIDS virus?
Rachel R.
Pittsburgh, PA.

Dear Dr. Cory:
My friends are lerning about
AIDS. Can you Help us?
Mean
Andria B.
Baltimore, MD

Dear Andria:

The letters A-I-D-S stand for Acquired Immune Deficiency Syndrome. A person with AIDS has been infected by a unique virus resulting in a pattern of unusual diseases that create a life-threatening health problem.

The AIDS virus attacks the immune system, which is the way our bodies fight germs to keep us healthy or make us better when we do get sick. A person without a functioning immune system may easily become infected with life-threatening diseases such as pneumonia, meningitis, and cancer.

The AIDS virus can be passed by an infected person if that person's blood or body fluids become mixed with another person's blood or body fluids. This typically occurs through sexual contact or through the sharing of intravenous needles and syringes used for "shooting" drugs. Some people have gotten the disease in other ways such as by receiving blood transfusions from someone who had the AIDS virus.

There is presently no cure for AIDS and no vaccine to prevent it. The best form of protection is learning the ways the virus is passed, and then avoiding those practices. Because AIDS is most commonly transmitted through sexual contact with an infected person, or through contaminated needles and syringes, you can avoid AIDS by saying "No" to sex and drugs.

34

Dear Rachel:

Some people remain apparently well after infection with the AIDS virus. They may have no physically apparent symptoms of illness. A person with AIDS-related complex (ARC) has a condition caused by the AIDS virus in which the patient also tests positive for AIDS infection and has a specific type of illness. However, ARC patients' symptoms are often less severe than those with the disease we call classic AIDS. Signs and symptoms of ARC may include: loss of appetite, weight loss, fever, night sweats, skin rashes, diarrhea, tiredness, lack of resistance to infection, or swollen lymph nodes. These are also signs and symptoms of many other diseases, and if noted a physician should be consulted.

Only a qualified health professional can diagnose AIDS, which is the result of the progress of infection by the AIDS virus. Some signs and symptoms of Pneumocystis carinii pneumonia, one of the diseases that a person with AIDS becomes more vulnerable to, are a persistent cough and fever, associated with shortness of breath or difficult breathing. Or a person with AIDS may develop multiple purplish blotches and bumps on the skin that may be a sign of Kaposi's sarcoma (a type of cancer).

AIDS patients are susceptible to many infectious diseases and also die from them. They can come down with tuberculosis, histoplasmosis, or toxoplasmosis, and even a salmonella infection can be very serious for an AIDS patient.

The AIDS virus may also attack the nervous system and cause delayed damage to the brain. This damage may take years to develop, and the symptoms may show up as memory loss, loss of coordination, partial paralysis, or mental disorder. These symptoms may occur alone or with other symptoms mentioned earlier.

Dear Doctor Cory:
What is a stroke?
Anne S   Tampa, Fla.

Dear Anne:

A stroke is a type of injury to the brain where the blood to a particular part of the brain is suddenly cut off. Strokes usually result from a narrowing or a complete closing of one of the blood vessels supplying blood to the brain. The nerves that control our voluntary motions, our speech, our temperature, our vision, our sensation of pain, and our touch all pass through the brain. When a stroke occurs, these nerves may be damaged.

A stroke can cause death, but more often the person makes a good recovery and is able to lead a normal life.

High blood pressure is one of the main causes of strokes. At any age it is important to avoid being overweight, smoking, and certain items in our diet such as salt that are associated with high blood pressure. By avoiding these in our younger years, we may be able to prevent high blood pressure from occurring when we are older—thus helping to prevent strokes.

35

Dear Dr. Cory,
How do people have heartatacks? and how do they happen?
Terri S.
Delavan Mn.

Dear Dr. Cory,
My Grandma died because she had diabetes. What causes this?

Bryan P.
Ottawa, Ontario

Dear Bryan:

Diabetes is a medical condition that is caused when the pancreas ceases or slows production of a substance called insulin.

Insulin is needed for the body to properly use sugar (or glucose). Sugar is necessary to provide the energy the body needs to think, run, play, and work. To put it bluntly, without insulin, the body cannot function, and it dies.

There are two types of diabetes. Diabetes Type I most often develops in children and young adults. It requires that insulin be given artificially, by injection, to allow the body to utilize glucose and function. Supplying the insulin artificially is a treatment, but it is *not* a cure; the body does not begin to make its own insulin.

Diabetes Type II usually develops in people after the age of 35, but can occur in younger persons. This type can sometimes be controlled with diet and exercise. In this type of diabetes, the body makes some insulin, but not quite enough to regulate all the body's needs. Type II diabetes may go away if the person loses excess weight. Occasionally, pills taken by mouth encourage the body to make more insulin.

If either type of diabetes is not treated promptly and properly, serious complications will develop. Smoking, in particular, can make diabetic complications worse.

The causes of Type I and Type II diabetes are unknown. However, there are several factors which may help to cause this disease. First of all, if anyone in the family has had diabetes, it increases the risk for other family members at some point to develop it. (However, it is not a contagious disease.) So, it may be hereditary. Researchers are also beginning to think that a fault in the immune system (the system that fights disease in our body) may be a factor in causing the disease. This theory is supported by the observation that diabetes often begins just after a viral illness, such as chickenpox, the flu, or a bad cold. Diabetes also seems to follow times of unusual stress.

Obesity is a major factor for consideration in Type II diabetes. Women also have higher incidence of diabetes, while pregnant.

36

Dear Terri:

Your heart is an organ made of muscle tissue that acts as a pump to supply blood to the body. Your heart also needs blood pumped to its own muscle tissue, to keep the muscle strong and healthy.

There are two main blood vessels that supply the heart with blood. They are called the right and left coronary arteries. The blood supply to the heart shuts off when one of these arteries becomes plugged. This causes a heart attack and that is why heart attacks are often called coronaries. The part of the heart without blood begins to die.

When one coronary artery becomes plugged, eventually the smaller vessels of the other artery take over the work of the plugged artery. So a person who has had a heart attack needs immediate medical care and must be closely watched until those vessels have a chance to start helping the heart. If the second artery can carry on the work of the first artery, the person recovers. Fortunately, this often happens, due to improved medical care.

There are a number of factors that increase a person's risk of heart attacks. Some of these factors a person has little control over, such as age, sex, and heredity. Heart attacks are common in older men who have a family history of heart disease. However, there are many factors that a person can control. They include: high blood pressure, cigarette smoking, high blood cholesterol (which comes from eating a diet high in fat but low in fiber), stress and the inability to cope with it, obesity, diabetes, and lack of exercise.

Dear Dr. Cory,
My grandmother has a high blood pressure. How can she slow it down?

Brian H.
West Mifflin, PA.

Dear Brian:

Your grandmother has a very common condition, also called hypertension. There are several things she can do to help lower her blood pressure. She can lose weight (if necessary), stop smoking, and decrease the amount of sodium or salt in her diet.

Often these simple measures, if strictly followed, are all that is needed to control mild increases in the blood pressure. Medication can effectively treat those people who have ongoing difficulty with hypertension.

High blood pressure causes the heart to work harder, so it is important to treat this condition. Encourage your grandmother to follow her doctor's advice.

37

Dear Dr. Cory:

My aunt has polio in her leg. Could you please give me some information about this disease?

Emily F.
Westlake, Ohio

Dear Dr. Cory,

What is Cancer and How do you get it?

Kelly C
age 10 Woodland Hills Calif.

Dear Emily:

Polio is caused by a virus that gets into the nerve cells of the spinal cord and damages them. Sometimes this damage is so severe that some part of the body is left without controls.

If the nerves that control the legs were severely damaged, the person might have to wear braces, walk with crutches, or use a wheelchair. That is what happened to President Franklin D. Roosevelt, who contracted polio as a young man. Not all people infected with polio are paralyzed.

Was your aunt a child or young adult in the early 1950s? If so, she may have been a victim of an epidemic of polio that spread through the United States in 1952. By 1955 polio vaccine was available, and today the disease is quite rare. It is very important that all children receive the vaccine, to prevent another epidemic of this tragic and preventable disease.

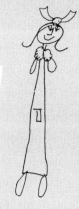

38

Dear Kelly:

Cancer happens in a person's body when a cell begins to grow and divide much too quickly. Your body is made up of millions of cells of different types, each too small to see without a microscope. When cancer causes cells to increase much too rapidly they can grow into a tumor that spreads and injures the normal cells near it.

Scientists have come up with many ideas about what causes cancer, but there is much they do not know. Probably we will learn that there are different causes of different cancers.

Because we don't know all about what causes cancer, it is very difficult to treat the disease. Doctors can sometimes remove tumors by surgery, and there are many medications that doctors use on people with cancer to shrink a tumor or even, sometimes, to kill it. There are many different kinds of cancer, so the treatment varies depending on the type of cancer.

Dear Dr. Cory,
How can you get cancer and how can you prevent it?

Erica Z.
Shelton, Connecticut

Dear Erica:

It is believed that most cancers have external causes. Therefore, they should be preventable. The causes of some cancers have been fairly obvious for some time, but—unfortunately—for most cancers the causes are not so obvious. Generally the air we breathe, the water we drink, the food we eat, the way we prepare our food, our contact with infectious diseases and other living creatures, radiation, and our lifestyles all have a role in the causes of cancer. Many cancers can be cured if caught and treated right away. Some cancers can be prevented by avoiding their causes.

For instance, cigarette smoking causes the majority of lung cancers. Smokeless tobacco and snuff greatly increase the chance of mouth, larynx, and throat cancer. Researchers are finding that it may be even tougher to quit chewing tobacco or snuff than to quit smoking cigarettes. If young children start this habit they could be addicted for life. Obese people have a greater risk of getting colon, breast, and uterine cancer. Breast, colon, and prostate cancer may be more likely to develop in those who have a high-fat diet. Heavy drinkers of alcohol have a higher number of mouth, larynx, throat, and liver cancers.

You can reduce your chance of developing cancer by:
• not smoking
• not using smokeless tobacco or snuff
• avoiding obesity
• cutting down on total fat intake
• eating more high-fiber foods such as whole grain cereals, bran, fruit, and vegetables
• including foods rich in vitamins A and C in your daily diet
• including cruciferous vegetables (cabbage, broccoli, brussels sprouts, cauliflower) in your diet
• eating only moderate amounts of salt, smoked, and nitrate-cured foods

Exposure to the sun is being found to be directly related to skin cancer. Protection from the sun is strongly recommended to avoid skin cancer.

39

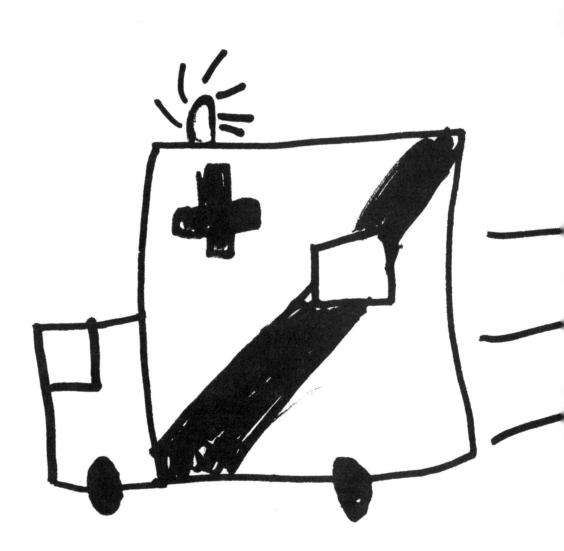

Accidents and Injuries

Broken bones, skinned knees, cuts, insect stings. These are the accidental injuries most children experience. They are delighted to find that the damage can be repaired.

The broken leg or arm will be good as new some day, and fresh pink skin will appear from under the ugly scab on the knee.

Children are familiar with the concept of "broken" and "fixed" from babyhood. Favorite toys break. Mother's treasured dish breaks, when the child drops it. The car breaks down and Daddy takes it to the garage to be fixed.

It is quite logical for the child to view the doctor as the "fixer" of whatever part of the body "broke." The doctor's stitches, cast, and splints are counterpart to the glue, tape, and wire Daddy uses when he fixes a broken toy.

Sometimes the child is so impressed by the doctor's skill at "fixing" that he or she decides to become a doctor, too, and I receive letters like this:

Dear Dr. Cory:

How does it feel being a Doctor? And how do you put stitches in? I want to be a Doctor. I want to learn to put stitches in just like you. That's why!

Angela K., age 7

Dear Angela:

I hope you make it! I shall welcome you as a colleague!

Cory SerVaas, M.D.

Dear Dr. Cory:
What should you do if a baby
drowend or couden't breath?
I have a two year old sister
who almost drowend, her name
is Maria. what should you do?
                    Michelle M.
                    Scottsdale, Arizona

Dear Michelle:

If you are ever in this situation I hope there will be an adult nearby, and I hope the adult has learned how to do CPR on a small child.

Call the nearest adult. Then go to the telephone and call your community's emergency number for medical assistance.

When a person stops breathing because of drowning or choking and his or her heart stops beating, the flow of blood to the brain stops. Blood must begin to flow to the brain again within four to six minutes, or the brain may be permanently damaged.

The letters CPR stand for Cardio (heart) Pulmonary (lungs) Resuscitation. A person who has learned CPR can help in this situation by first clearing the air passage of the victim, then blowing air into his lungs. Next, the person pushes on the victim's chest so as to help his heart beat, and get blood circulating again. When this is done correctly it can keep the victim alive until help arrives, or until he or she begins breathing again.

Since you may someday be in an emergency situation like this when there is no other person present, it would be an excellent idea for you to learn to perform CPR, just as soon as you are old enough. Contact your local American Red Cross or the American Heart Association office, and ask when and where the training is given, and how old you need to be to enroll.

Dear Dr. Cory,
What do you do to
treat a burn?

Monica H.

Bethlehem, Pa.

42

Dear Monica:

Immediately put the burned part in cold water, or let cold tap water run over it. If you're outdoors you can use water from the garden hose, if it is cool. If it is a first degree burn (skin reddened) continue the cold water treatment for 10 minutes; no other treatment may be needed. Do *not* put butter or any other grease or ointment on the burn, as that will only slow healing.

If the burn is more severe (blistered skin, crusted or blackened skin) or if the burn is on the head, hands, feet, or genitals, the person should be seen by a doctor as soon as possible. Use the cold water treatment first, then cover the burned part of the body with a clean sheet dampened with cold water, for transportation to the doctor's office or hospital. Do not use any grease or ointment. Do not cover the burn with dry gauze or cloth, as it would stick to the burn and cause more damage.

Burns can be very painful and leave ugly scars. All the more reason to *prevent* them. One good rule: Keep matches and cigarette lighters where small children can't get at them.

Dear Susan:

Fainting is the temporary loss of consciousness caused by a lack of oxygen in the brain. The doctors' name for this is "syncope." Fainting may be caused by exhaustion, heat, lack of air, weakness, or by some strong emotion like happiness, or fear, or shock at the sight of blood. Some people faint more easily than others.

A person who is about to faint may say he feels weak or dizzy. His face may be pale, or his lips begin to turn blue. The pulse may be weak and rapid. There may be cold sweat on the person's forehead. The person may have trouble breathing. Have him sit down and hold his head between his knees, or lie flat on the floor. In either position, more blood carrying oxygen will flow to the brain, and the person will soon recover.

If the person remains unconscious for more than a short period of time it is possible that something very serious has happened. Call for emergency help or take the person to the nearest hospital.

43

Dear John:

Pain is a very important signal that lets you know when something is wrong with your body.

Can you imagine what might happen if you did *not* feel pain? You might put your hand on a hot stove and leave it there until your hand was seriously burned. You might cut your foot on a sharp stone and not notice until you had lost a great deal of blood.

Fortunately there are nerves in almost every part of your body, and when there is an injury, the nerves very quickly carry the pain signal to the brain, telling you that you must do something to protect or heal your body.

Many diseases begin with pain, such as a headache or stomach-ache. These kinds of pain are also signals telling you that something is wrong.

Dear Dr. Cory.

Why do you feel pain when you ~~hurt yourself~~ hurt yourself?

John L
Roch, N.Y.

Dear Dr. Cory
My friend broke her arm by jumping off a swing. ~~How~~ She fell wrong. How could that happen?

Becky B
Spring valley, Minnesota

44

Dear Becky:

What happened to your friend is not at all unusual. Your bones are strong, and they are even slightly flexible so they can bend a little, but no single bone is strong enough to support your entire weight when you land with a sudden jolt—as when you fall out of a tree, or from a high swing, or off a porch roof. If you land on one outstretched arm, that arm is likely to break.

What's the right way to fall? If you have a choice, fall feet first, with your knees bent. Your bent legs can act like a spring to absorb the shock of your fall and let you down easy, so you are less likely to break bones.

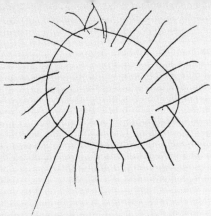

Dear Dr. Cory:
When I broke my leg the doctor said it was a compound fracture, and that was the worst kind. What's the other kind, and why is it better?

Danielle B.
Milwaukee, Wisc.

Dear Danielle:

In a simple fracture, bones are broken but the skin is not broken. In a compound fracture both bone and skin are broken, so there is bleeding, and the danger that dirt and germs can get inside the body and cause infection. Some doctors now call this an "open" fracture.

A simple fracture can be very painful but it is easier to treat and it will usually heal faster than a compound fracture.

Dear Dr. Cory:
My friend Jenny broke her arm. The doctor said it was a "hairline" fracture. What does this mean?

Mandy H.
Manville, N.J.

Dear Mandy:

A fracture is a break in a bone. A hairline fracture is a partial fracture in a bone, a crack as thin as a hairline. Adult bones are strong and hard. Children's bones are more flexible and capable of bending, almost like a tree branch. So sometimes, because of this elasticity, a child's bone can crack without actually breaking.

This type of fracture may not be noticeable on an X-ray until several weeks after it happens. Often, the best treatment is avoiding the use of the limb, or bone, in which the fracture occurred.

45

Dear Dr. Cory,
How do your bones mend when they are broken?
Kevin W.

Dear Kevin:

The most important thing for you to remember about bone is that it is not brittle like an old dead stick, but that it is *living*. It is made of cells, just like your muscles or the other organs of your body. The things that make bones hard are calcium and other minerals deposited in the cells. Your bones can even bend (just a little). When a bone is bent too far, it breaks. But right away a thick jellylike substance starts forming between the broken ends. Calcium and other minerals begin to be deposited in the jelly, and the ends of the bone are "woven" together. Gradually the cells of the bone ends grow into the broken area and new bone forms. The healing process usually takes about six weeks, and the bone must be kept very still during this time. That's why your doctor usually puts a cast or splint on a bone while it's healing.

Dear Doctor Cory,
How come went you brake a bone they put a cast on it because it gives you cramps?
Rachel D.
Pine Brook, NJ

Dear Rachel:

Whenever a part of your body is not well, rest is usually one of the needed treatments in order to get healthy again. Therefore, when a bone is broken (or fractured) it is very important to let the broken bone "rest." A cast helps to do this. Also, wearing a cast should make the pain from the fracture go away quicker and the bone heal better.

Every once in a while, while you are wearing a cast, the muscles around and near the fracture might develop cramps. The cramps usually last only for short while. If not, the pain can be relieved by taking medicine prescribed by the doctor. If the pain is not helped by acetaminophen, or the pain is there most of the time, please call your doctor; your cast may need changing.

46

Dear Dr. Cory
I broke my leg once.
When the cast came off my leg was
weak. Why is that?

Allison M.
So. Glastonbury, Conn.

Dear Dr. Cory:
When you have a cut
with a scab on it, why
does it itch so much
when it is healing?

Kim B.
Chinchilla, Pennsylvania

Dear Allison:

Your leg became weak because you weren't using it. Any part of your body that isn't used regularly will deteriorate, which means becoming weak and helpless. On the other hand, exercise will make your body stronger.

You may have noticed that the injured leg was actually smaller than the other, because of shrinkage of the unused muscles while inside the cast.

I hope your doctor told you how to exercise so as to build up the strength of the injured leg gradually and safely, after the cast was removed, and the leg that was broken is now as good as new.

Dear Kim:

As your skin is healing and growing new cells, the skin around the injury stretches and pulls up around it. This tightening and stretching of the skin is what causes the itching sensation.

It is important to resist the urge to scratch and remove the scab. The healing occurs more quickly when the skin is protected by the scab. Removing the scab before it is ready to fall off causes irritation, not healing.

47

Dear Dr. Cory,

I am in second grade. I would like to ask you a question. When you have a cut, how does your skin grow back together?

Brandie J.
Chicago, Illinois

Dear Brandie:

Did you know that your skin doesn't really grow back together when you have a cut? It only seems that it does because you can't see how your cut actually heals.

Skin covers up your insides and keeps them from getting dirty or hurt. It can stretch, and it is always growing. Skin grows in a special way, though. It grows in layers. New skin doesn't grow on top of the old skin. New skin grows *underneath* the old skin. As new skin grows, it pushes up the layer above it. This layer pushes up the next one, and then the top layer comes off. You have probably seen someone whose skin was peeling because of a sunburn. What was peeling was the top layer.

The top layer of your skin is always coming off. Most of the time, you aren't aware of it because it comes off in tiny pieces. These pieces are so small that you can't see them unless you have a magnifying glass or microscope. These pieces are called cells, and cells make up your skin layers.

When you cut your skin, you cut through the layers. The layers underneath just keep on growing like they always do, and the top layer keeps falling off gradually. Soon, your cut is all gone, because new skin has grown in where the old, cut skin was. Most of the time, you can't even see where a cut has been.

48

Dear Dr. Cory:
How do you get blood blisters?
Holly J.
Emporia, Kansas

Dear Holly:

Blood blisters are caused by some sort of trauma to the skin, such as pinching or hitting. They are regular blisters, but they contain blood. A small blood vessel under the top layer of the skin has been broken due to the trauma and has bled into the blister that formed from the pressure of the injury. Blood blisters should not be opened because that only increases the possibility of infection. Usually they dry and peel away within one to two weeks.

Dear Dr. Cory,
How do you get bruises?
Sean K.
Wendell, North Carolina

Dear Sean:

When a certain part of your body, such as one of your arms or legs, hits an object, a bruise may result. A bruise is actually a form of bleeding, only it is bleeding under the outer layer of skin into the inner skin. It causes a discoloration of the skin, but it does not break the skin. It is necessary sometimes to treat bruises with cold packs to reduce swelling; otherwise they just go away with time.

Dear Dr. Cory:
When you get a bump on your head, why do you get a bump, but if you bump your knee you get a bruise?
Hannah D.
Dallas, Texas

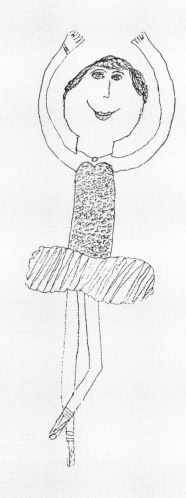

49

Dear Hannah:

When you bump your head you get a bump because of the hard bone under the skin. The blood forms a quick bump on top of the bone, under the skin, as it escapes from the damaged blood vessel. If you bump your knee the blood can spread under the skin and you will have a bruise.

The damage is the same, and the blood is released in the same way. The difference is in the ability of the blood to spread. The color you see depends on how deep the blood vessel is under the skin. The deeper the blood, the less likely you are to see the blood; you might just feel the bump.

Chapter 5

Children Ask Questions About

Their Appearance

Because of higher living standards and generally better nutrition, today's children are maturing at an earlier age. And, more than ever before, they are surrounded by media messages stressing the importance of appearance. The newest hairstyle. Designer jeans. A standard of physical beauty that includes a clear complexion and a slim figure.

Long before the teenage years when yesterday's parents expected these problems to surface, seven- and eight-year-olds study the images on the TV screen and then look in a mirror and are dissatisfied with what they see.

Freckles. Pimples. A wart or mole. Hair too curly or too straight. Hips and tummy too rounded to look good in skin-tight jeans or miniskirt. Even a tiny defect is disaster to a sensitive youngster who believes he or she will be judged solely on appearance.

Parents need to listen, and to offer help, when children voice these concerns. Professional help with skin problems, crooked teeth, or weight control can make a big difference. And the child who feels good about the way he or she looks will gain confidence and be a happier, more outgoing child.

Dear Dr. Cory,

Why are some people black (or as I see brown) and some people white (or as I see, peach-colored)?

Danielle L.
Anaheim, CA

Dear Danielle:

We have a substance in our skin called pigment, which is what makes our skin the color it is. The more pigment you have, the darker your skin. Some races of people have darker skin because of the climate where they—or their ancestors—lived. In very warm climates where the temperature is hot most of the time, the people who have lived there for thousands of years have darker skin as a protection from the sun. People who have lived in cooler climates for thousands of years have lighter skin.

So, you see, the color of the skin was the body's way of adapting to the area where the person lived. It's hard for us to remember, but until the last few hundred years, people rarely traveled far from where they, and their ancestors, were born. Due to this limited traveling, a group of people became very similar in their physical appearance and would share customs, language, and history. This group would then be called a "race."

Dear Dr. Cory,
What causes freckles?

Thank you,
Jessica W.
Riverview, Florida

Dear Jessica:

Freckles are formed when some skin cells produce more of a pigment called *melanin* than the surrounding cells. This tendency is hereditary. It is most noticeable in fair-skinned people (usually blonds or redheads). Suntanning tends to make the freckles show up more as the pigmented areas become much darker than the surrounding pale skin.

Freckles do not need to be treated. Using a good sunscreen lotion will help to keep the freckles from darkening over the summer.

52

Dear Dr. Cory,

My grandfather wears a hat when he goes out in the summertime, to keep from getting cancer. He says I should wear a hat too. I'd rather take my shirt off and get nice and brown all over. What do you think about hats and sunburns?

Brian R.
Kansas City, Missouri

Dear Brian:

I think your grandfather is right! He should wear a hat to protect his face and head from the sun, and you should wear a hat, too. (And a shirt.) We know now that a bad sunburn today may mean skin cancer later—maybe 50 to 60 years from now, when you're a senior citizen. Your grandfather may be having skin problems that are due to his having been out in the sun too much when he was a little boy.

Of course you won't want to wear a hat and shirt and long pants to protect your skin when you're on the beach, or around a pool, but you can use sunscreen. That's a cream or lotion you spread on your skin to filter out the harmful rays of the sun. Sunscreens have numbers that indicate how much protection they offer. Use a higher number if your skin is very sensitive, or if the sun is very bright; a lower number if your skin is less sensitive or the sun not so bright. Apply more sunscreen after swimming, as some will wash off.

53

. . . About Their Appearance

Dear Dr Cory: older how can
when you grow grow with you? O
your skin Does it stretch?

Melody H

Amboy   Indiana O

Dear Melody:

Yes, your skin can stretch, but not enough to accommodate your growth from baby to adult size. So your skin has to get larger, as the rest of you does.

Like other parts of the body, the skin is constantly renewing itself. Old cells die and flake off, new cells replace them. During growth years a special hormone circulates with the blood, signaling all body parts to produce extra cells, more than are needed for replacement. The extra cells make your bones and muscle tissue—and your skin—all grow larger.

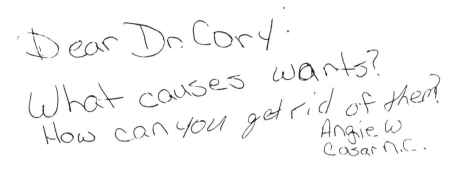

Dear Dr. Cory:
What causes warts?
How can you get rid of them?
Angie W
Casar N.C.

Dear Angie:

Warts are growths on the surface of the skin. They are caused by a certain type of virus. They are spread by person-to-person touching or sometimes by touching objects contaminated by the virus. Plantar warts are a type of wart that grows on the soles of the feet and sometimes on the palms of the hands. They are often painful. More than 50 percent of warts will disappear without treatment within two years. However, an untreated wart may spread to other areas of the body. Your doctor can prescribe a special medicine that will slowly reduce the wart. He can perform a special treatment in his office that is often a faster way to remove the wart. Unfortunately, neither treatment guarantees that the wart will not return.

Dear Dr. Cory:
What are moles?

Carrie P.

Saranac Lake, N.Y.

Dear Carrie:

A mole is a permanent discoloration of a small raised area of skin due to a change in the skin's *pigmentation. Pigment* gives the skin its color. This change in the skin's pigment causes the dark color of the mole.

If a person is born with a mole or if a mole covers a large portion of the body, the mole should be checked by a doctor. It is also important to watch for any changes in a mole. The change *may* be a sign of skin cancer.

Any mole that changes in size, shape, or color, or bleeds frequently, should be checked by a dermatologist (a skin doctor).

55

Dear Dr. Cory:
I have some questions about pimples.
Why do some kids have lots of them and some
not so many?

Elizabeth L
Kansas City, Missouri

Dear Elizabeth:

For one thing, if your parents had acne (that means having pimples) you are likely to have acne. We know that acne is often due to increased production of certain hormones. Heredity, stress, and fatigue may be factors in hormone production.

When there is more of the hormone present in the body, the skin glands produce more oil, and the oil glands are more likely to become plugged with oil, dead skin cells, and debris. When infection occurs, the result is a red, angry pimple.

Today we do not think that dirt or oil on the face, or the eating of certain foods like "junk food" and chocolate, have much to do with causing pimples.

Keeping the face clean is, however, a good idea, as this will help to keep pimples from becoming infected. For the same reason, don't squeeze or "pop" pimples with your fingers.

And staying away from junk food is a good idea, as it does not furnish you with all the things your body needs to grow. Junk food can lead to poor nutrition and obesity.

For more about pimples, read the next question and answer.

56

Dear Dr. Cory,

My friends always make fun of me because I have pimples. What causes them? I've tried alot of stuff but it does not work. What about accutane?

Geri D.
Summerfield, Kansas

Dear Geri:

You do not mention your age, but having pimples or acne is a skin condition that normally develops during the teenage years. Everyone has at some point some acne; it's just a matter of degree. Some lucky young people have just a mild or moderate case, while other cases are more severe.

There are many over-the-counter products for acne; some are very helpful, while others will not do much good. Your doctor can determine the kind of medication that will work best for your particular skin condition, or he will refer you to a dermatologist (skin doctor).

Accutane, which is sometimes used to treat severe cases of acne, is one of several prescription drugs that are known to cause birth defects. For this reason, it must be used only under the strict supervision of a doctor. It must not be used by females who are pregnant, or who might become pregnant while being treated.

Problems of babies born to mothers who took Accutane while pregnant include: hydrocephalus, microcephalus, abnormalities of the external ear, and cardiovascular abnormalities.

Most acne is due to increased hormone production which causes oil glands in the skin to produce too much oil, which plugs tiny ducts that open onto the skin's surface. However, pimples may be the sign of some other, more serious skin disorder, so you should consult a doctor.

Some young people are embarrassed by complexion problems. I hope you will be willing to get help!

57

Dear Heather:

The term "birthmark" may be used to describe several types of skin changes seen at or shortly after birth. Medical science still does not know what causes these birthmarks, and no one has yet discovered how to prevent them. Most are harmless.

One kind of birthmark is a mole or neves. These may be raised and very dark. Often the treatment of choice is to remove moles of this kind, as they have an increased risk of future development of a serious type of skin cancer called malignant melanoma.

There are many other kinds of birthmarks. Some are purplish or reddish colorations of the skin that appear on the child's face or the back of the neck. Ones that are raised and red are called "strawberry marks." These kinds usually go away, naturally, and do not require treatment.

If a birthmark is unsightly or in an irritating spot, where it frequently bleeds or becomes infected, one should see a doctor about the possibility of having it removed surgically. Another possibility is covering it with makeup matched to your skin color.

Any mole or mark on the skin that changes in size, shape or color, or frequently bleeds, should be examined by a doctor. These changes are sometimes early signs of skin cancer.

58

Dear Dr. Cory:
Why does my older sister have dimples? She hates them. Is there any way to get rid of them?

Gabrielle E.
Houston, Texas

Dear Gabrielle:

Your sister was born with the features that make her who she is, such as the color of her hair and eyes, the shape of her face, and how tall she will be when she is grown. Dimples are features of her face that she was born with, and they are perfectly normal.

Dimples are different and distinctive. Sometimes having a facial feature that is different makes us want to change, to be more like everyone else, or to be "prettier." It is important to realize that being different is special, and to take pride in the fact that each of us has a unique role in life. Liking ourselves isn't always easy, but when we do, it gives us confidence.

Have your sister do a little research on other people with dimples. She'll be surprised to see how many people are blessed with this special skin crease!

59

Dear Dr. Cory,
Why do some twins look alike
and some twins don't?
Jane B
Cincinnati, Ohio

Dear Jane:

There are two kinds of twins: identical twins, and fraternal twins.

The identical twins are from one sperm and one egg. After fertilization takes place the egg splits into two parts, and each part develops into a baby. This means that the twins will be the same sex (two boys or two girls) and that they will have the same genetically determined characteristics. This is the reason they look alike, talk alike, and usually do things the same way. One thing that will be different is fingerprints—they will be similar but not exactly the same.

The fraternal twins are from two separate sperm and two separate eggs that just happen to be fertilized at the same time in the mother's womb. Their genetically determined characteristics will vary, as ordinary brothers and sisters vary. They may be of the same sex, or one girl and one boy. Basically, fraternal twins are brothers and sisters who differ from other brothers and sisters only in growing together inside the mother's body and being born at or near the same time.

Dear Dr. Cory,
Why are babies'
eyes blue when they
are born?
Carol T.
Brookings, Oregon.

Dear Carol:

The eyes of most light-skinned babies are blue at birth because there is only a small amount of melanin (the pigment that gives color to eyes, hair, and skin) in the eyes. Pigment continues to develop as a baby grows. The final color of the baby's eyes depends on the amount of pigment deposited there, determined by the baby's parents, i.e. heredity. If only a little pigment is deposited, the eyes will remain blue. When more pigment develops the eyes appear brown. Changes in a baby's eye color may be noticeable for several weeks.

60

Dear Dr. Cory,
   Why do some people have green eyes and some blue and brown and hazel.

Sincerely,
Heather G.
Glendale, Arizona

Dear Heather:

The color of a person's eyes is inherited from his parents. This is due to the genes that are passed from the parents to the child. Some genes are stronger than others and if the stronger gene, also known as a dominant gene, is passed on the child will have that color of eyes. On the other hand if only the weaker gene, known as a recessive gene, is passed then the child will have eyes of a different color.

Dear Dr. Cory:
   How do our eyes get their color and why does the color sometimes change? My eyes are sometimes blue and sometimes green.

Janelle B.
El Paso, Texas

Dear Janelle:

Eyes, skin, and hair color are inherited from your parents. Heredity determines how much pigment or color is produced in the iris of the eye. Eyes with no pigment are pink, like those of a white rabbit. Eyes with a small amount of pigment are blue, and those with much pigment are brown. Eye color may change as more pigment forms in the iris. Hair color may also change as it grows.

Eyes may appear to be a different color if they are observed under different colored lights.

61

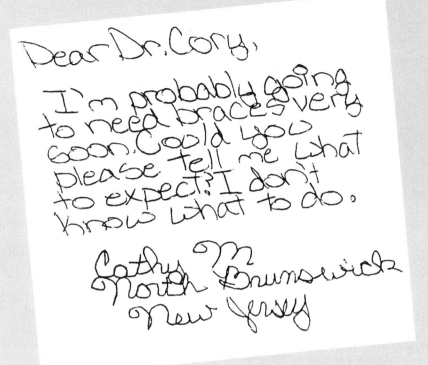

Dear Dr. Cory,

I'm probably going to need braces very soon. Could you please tell me what to expect? I don't know what to do.

Cathy M
North Brunswick
New Jersey

Dear Cathy:

Braces are an important advance in modern dentistry. Correcting an improper bite when you are young can mean a lifetime of better oral health and improved chewing, as well as a prettier smile! The dentist uses braces to help the teeth be in the proper places, and to help the jaw grow.

At first, braces can be uncomfortable. They will feel tight for a few weeks, but this gets better quickly. Before you know it, your braces won't hurt at all.

Be careful not to chew very hard candy, candy apples, nuts, or any other very hard foods, so your braces won't break. And be sure to brush your teeth after every meal, with or without braces!

Dear Dr. Cory,

How do you get cavities?

Your friend,
Sara R
Ellwood City, Pa

Dear Sara:

Cavities in teeth are usually the result of poor diet and eating too many sweets. Flossing and brushing your teeth carefully, to keep them clean, helps to prevent cavities. If possible, floss and brush after every meal. If you can't brush after a meal or snack, drink water or rinse your mouth with water.

Also important: See your dentist regularly. Then, if you do get cavities, he can fix them while they are still small.

Dear Dr. Cory
    Can you help me. I
don't brush my teeth
everyday. Its begging
to be a big habbit.
                Trisha A

Dear Trisha:

The fact that you wrote this
letter tells me that you can
help yourself, because you know
you *should* brush more often, and
you're thinking about it. Now's the
time to start a new habit of
brushing (and flossing) your teeth,
not just once a day, but twice or
more often. After each meal, if
possible. You will soon learn to love
the clean, fresh taste that's left in
your mouth after you brush.

Dear Dr. Cory
    I am 11 years old and my sister
is nine. She is towo years younger
than me, but she is taller! What
can I do?

                    Bobby J.
                Des Moines, Iowa

63

Dear Bobby:

You can be patient! Just wait,
and in a few years you will
catch up with her and then
probably grow taller. Girls may
begin to experience the physical
changes of puberty as early as
age nine and they may begin a
spurt of rapid growth due to the
increase of sex hormone
production. Boys more often begin
growing up at age 12 or later. There
are, therefore, several years during
which girls may be as tall or taller
than boys of the same age or older,
as in your case. But don't worry;
this will pass.

. . . About Their Appearance

Dear Lisa:

This is a response caused by the autonomic nervous system. This part of the nervous system is responsible for actions that the body does automatically. This includes functions of the glands (such as the sweat and saliva glands), smooth muscle tissue (such as the muscles used for digestion), and the heart. It also includes the skin's reaction of goose bumps, which usually occurs as a reaction to cold or an emergency situation such as fright. Certain muscles, called *arrector pili* muscles, are attached to the hair shafts under the skin. In cold or frightening situations these muscles contract. This causes the hair shafts to straighten, the hairs to rise, and the little bumps around the hair to rise on the skin.

64

Dear Jessica:

The hair you see is made from cells that have died. The new hair cells grow from a follicle in the skin or scalp. The follicle is a group of special cells in the skin or scalp that form hair. Each follicle has tiny blood vessels that supply nutrition and cause the hair to grow. The hair of the scalp grows an average of five to six inches each year.

Whether someone's hair is curly or straight depends on how the hair grows. Straight hair tends to be round, while curly hair tends to be flat.

The color, texture and curliness of hair are inherited characteristics, determined by the genes.

Dear Dr. Cory,

My hair is straight as a bone. My mom tries to curl it. This summer she tried to curl it by leaving the curlers in for a week. But it did not curl! What can I do? Should I wash it everyday? Should I take vitamins?

Karen H.
Villisca, Iowa

Dear Karen:

Can you believe that we have had letters from girls who are unhappy because their hair is curly? We have. You asked if you could take any vitamins to make your hair curl. I don't believe you could, but you could certainly eat a lot of good foods that will make your hair shine and glisten. A good diet shows up in healthy hair.

When I was a child and lived in Iowa on a farm, our cats would sometimes get into the chickens' nests and eat the eggs. My parents could tell when the cats were doing this because their fur would get thick and glistening. I'm telling you this only because it illustrates that good diet does make beautiful hair.

As far as the curling, your mother may, when you are older, be happy to get a permanent wave for you to give you curly hair. In the meantime, enjoy your hair the way it is and eat right to keep it looking healthy. It may also help you feel better to remember that many curly-haired girls want straight hair. In fact, some people buy a hair product in drug stores that will straighten their curls!

65

Breakfast

Chapter 6

Children Ask Questions About

Nutrition and Weight Control

Weight control is the subject of many of the letters we receive from young readers. Some letters are from children (mostly girls) who say they are too thin and want to gain weight, but most are from boys and girls who describe themselves as "chubby" and who want to lose weight.

Some—usually girls—seem overly concerned about a very few pounds. We'd like to reassure them, tell them that the perfect weight for one human being isn't necessarily right for another, even if they're the same age and height. Body types differ. The way we utilize food differs. Both body and metabolism will change as the child grows. The one who is too thin today may be overweight tomorrow, and vice versa.

But for others the concern and the problem are very real. Childhood obesity is a tragedy that almost inevitably leads to adult obesity and a life of unhappiness if bad eating habits are not unlearned. I hope we can help the children who know they have a problem and want to change.

Dear Dr. Cory:

What does nutrition have to do with your health?

Christina D.
Seaford, New York

Dear Dr. Cory:

When people lose pounds, where do the pounds go?

Annie V.
Mentor, Ohio

Dear Christina:

Nutrition has everything to do with your health! You may have heard the statement that "you are what you eat;" well, it's true. Doctors are finding more and more illnesses that are caused by bad eating habits. For example, cancer of the intestine is being linked to the highly refined sugar diet Americans have been eating for the past decades. Doctors have found that if the diet includes more fiber, the incidence of cancer of the intestine is much lower.

Your body is a very delicate "machine," and food is what keeps it going. If you want it to last longer you must take good care of it, just as you would your toys to make them last longer. So feed your body the good things it needs to give you a long life. Eat a diet that is low in sugar and fat, and high in fiber.

Dear Annie:

That is a very good question! First, let's find out where pounds come from. When you eat, your food is used as energy by your body. We measure the amount of energy in our food in calories. Usually our bodies use up the energy in the food we eat every day when we work, go to school, play, and move about. Our bodies also need this energy to function, so we will stay healthy. But when you eat too much food, your body stores the calories, or energy that is not used, and the amount stored is measured in pounds.

When you are very active, as when you are exercising, your body uses up more calories. If you are not eating *enough* calories for the energy your body needs, your body uses the energy it has stored. This is when you lose weight. You can't *see* the pounds you have lost because your body has used them in energy.

68

Dear Dr. Cory:

My sister doesn't eat right food. She only eats Junk. Will it hurt her?

Douglas C.
Okinawa, Japan

Dear Dr. Cory:

What will happen if you eat too much candy at one time?

Valerie M.
Bronx, New York

Dear Douglas:

Yes, poor diet will hurt your sister, sooner or later, in one way or another. People who do not eat the right foods become malnourished, which means they become weak and tired, they get sick more often than people who eat a good diet, and they do not perform as well as they should in school or at play.

"Junk foods" do not contain the vitamins and minerals that are needed to make the body work properly. Some junk foods contain large amounts of fat and salt, which can lead to heart attacks and high blood pressure. Other junk foods contain large amounts of sugar which has also been shown to cause heart attacks as well as blood disorders and psychological problems. Junk food can make you overweight.

Good diet is absolutely essential if a person is to lead a happy and healthy life.

69

Dear Valerie:

Eating too much of any food is not a good thing. Most people who are overweight are so because they eat too much and don't exercise enough. But it is particularly foolish to eat too much candy because it has so many calories and very little food value. You get full on something that doesn't supply your body with the nutrients it needs to grow and to fight off disease. Candy also is bad for your teeth. The chances for cavities increase when large amounts of sugar, especially sticky candy, are eaten.

Hi
   My name is Danielle. What
I like to know is: Dear Doctor
Corey how can you stop
eating junk food?
P.S. write back soon.
                    Danielle W.
                    Indianapolis

Dear Doctor
   Cory:
What causes
your stomach
to growl?

        Kim O.
   Danbury, Conn.

Dear Danielle:

Keep your tummy filled with carrot sticks, celery, apples, pears, raisins, radishes, popcorn, whole-wheat-bread sandwiches, and high-fiber cereals. You will find you have no appetite for junk food if you eat plenty of the good things and drink plenty of water, lemonade, and your favorite pure fruit juices.

   You will of course be thirsty when you are hot and come in from playing. That's the time to just say no to colas and soda pop by hurrying to get yourself cool water or fruit juice to drink.

70

Dear Kim:

The sound you call "growling" usually occurs when your stomach is empty but ready to begin its work of digesting food. If you smell food cooking, or even think about food, a signal is sent to your stomach. The digestive juices start to flow, and the empty stomach begins the rolling and churning motion that will mix food with the juices. This gives you a feeling you identify as hunger pangs, and if there is a little air or gas in the churning stomach you may hear a rumbling noise.

Dear Dr. Cory:

How do you get burps?
My parents say that when
you eat too much you burp.

Is that true?

Cynthia.
Allentown Pa.

Dear Cynthia:

Burps (or belching) is caused by air or gas escaping from the stomach. It makes a noise as it passes through the larynx or voice box.

There are several different ways air or gas can get into the stomach. Sometimes when you eat too fast you swallow air along with the food. Some foods such as beans and corn contain pockets of air that are released as the food is digested. Other foods give off a gas as they are digested. Colas and other carbonated drinks contain large amounts of gas (that's why they bubble).

When gas builds up in the stomach it will eventually escape through the esophagus, causing what you call a burp.

71

Dear Doctor Cory,
I have problems with stomach aches. I have them almost all the time. Do you know whats wrong.
            Sign Dearly,
            Jenny L.
            Yukon, Okla.

Dear Jenny:

There are many causes of stomachaches. The most common is the irritation of the stomach by certain foods. Your stomach will ache in order to let you know not to eat that food again.

Does your stomach ache after breakfast? If so, did your breakfast include fruit juice? Some people cannot easily digest certain fruit juices such as apple juice, and drinking these juices can cause a stomachache.

You can also get a stomachache if you run or play hard too soon after eating.

Stomachaches can occur when you are ill with the flu or other diseases. And when people develop ulcers, which are sores inside the stomach, they often get very painful stomachaches.

It's normal to have a stomach-ache once in a while, for one of these reasons or another, but if you are having stomachaches several times a week or almost every day, you should see a doctor and discuss this problem.

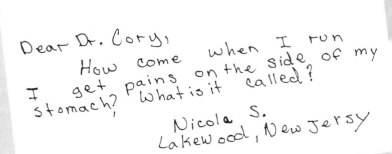

Dear Dr. Cory,
How come when I run I get pains on the side of my stomach? What is it called?
            Nicola S.
            Lakewood, New Jersy

Dear Nicola:

I often get this question from my readers. Running causes some stretching and squeezing of the stomach and intestinal muscles. A decreased supply of blood to a muscle causes a muscle spasm (the uncontrollable squeezing of a muscle). The muscle spasm causes the pain, which we call stomach cramps. This can be a problem, particularly after eating. The stomach and intestinal muscles are already busy digesting food. Any

72

Dear Dr. Cory:

Some of the kids in the neighborhood were wondering how and why we get diarrhea. Please answer this question.

Carla and Stacy
Aurora, Illinois

Dear Carla and Stacy:

Viral or bacterial infections are frequently the cause of diarrhea. These infections can be picked up from poor hygiene (not washing hands well after using the bathroom and before eating) or from contaminated food and water. At other times diarrhea may be due to a food intolerance such as *lactose intolerance*. Lactose is the main sugar in milk. Some people are unable to digest it and thus have bloating, cramping, and diarrhea when they drink milk or eat milk products.

Whatever the cause, diarrhea occurs when the intestine is unable to absorb nutrients and fluids normally. So one of the big concerns in treating diarrhea is making sure the person stays well hydrated by drinking plenty of fluids. However, only certain fluids—especially clear fluids—are helpful for a person with diarrhea. It's best to stay in touch with your doctor while recovering from diarrhea.

73

form of exercise, such as running or swimming, means more blood is needed for the stomach and intestinal muscles, which puts more stress on this particular part of the body. That is why it is best to rest after eating before doing any strenuous exercise.

This is just one example of your body sending you a message. If your side aches from running, rest until it feels better. Listen to your body.

Dear, Doctor Cory

I have a BIG !!!!!!!promblem. Your probly skinny as a cat

I'm as big as a pig. I don't eat much!   ! ⚫_ PLEASE TELL ME

HOW TO BE SKINNY   Sarah H

          Centralai Kansas

Dear Sarah:

If you are overweight, I am glad that you want to do something about it now. Often an overweight child becomes an overweight adult.

Obesity can be harmful to your health in many ways, physically as well as psychologically. Becoming an overweight adult can greatly affect your career, your marriage, and your overall lifestyle.

Some general guidelines in losing weight are:

• Talk to your doctor and set a goal weight. Check your progress with him or her regularly.

• Eat only when you are hungry.

• Avoid eating when you are bored or upset. Instead, do some type of activity such as jumping rope, bicycle riding, swimming, or playing a musical instrument.

• Look at your present eating habits. Watch out for those that involve eating more food and using less energy, such as snacking while watching TV. Not only do the programs and advertisements promote eating, but also it's easy to lose track when in front of the television of how much food you're consuming.

• Determine how much is eaten at meals and snack times. Eliminate second and third helpings of high-calorie foods like breads. Your parents can help you with this.

• Avoid snacks completely or have only low calorie ones, such as fruits or vegetables. It's best if snack foods are not even purchased. Then you and your family can't even be tempted. Even if other family members don't need to lose weight, they could probably improve their eating habits.

• Use low-fat milk and dairy products. Trim excess fat from meat. Bake, broil, or steam foods instead of frying them. Limit the use of margarine, salad oil or dressing, and sugar.

• Become involved in a regular exercise program. If team sports don't interest you, try swimming, gymnastics or tennis.

74

Dear Dr. Cory,

How can I gain some weight? I can eat and eat and eat but can not gain no weight I have been that way all my life I'm only 11 years old and weigh only 65 pounds and I am sinny minny PLEASE write Back and TELL ME

Your friend,
Shana S

P.S. Hope it works

Dear Dr. Cory,

Is pizza good to eat for breakfast?

Katie M
Billings, Montana

Dear Shana:

Differences in body metabolism—that is, the ways our bodies work—make it easy for some people to gain weight while others eat a lot and stay thin. It is not unusual for young people to be underweight and then change, gaining weight more easily as they get older. So you should continue to eat properly, getting a wide variety of different foods, including lots of fruits and vegetables. Don't overeat, or eat lots of sweets, as they won't help you gain weight but will cause other problems later.

If you are truly concerned, or if you have other problems such as becoming tired quickly, dizziness, weakness of the joints, or dark circles under your eyes, better see a doctor. He or she may prescribe vitamins or suggest a special diet that will help you gain weight and feel better.

75

Dear Katie:

When you wake up in the morning your body has been without food for as many as 12 hours and it needs a well-balanced meal that provides the different nutrients needed for good health. Pizza alone cannot accomplish this.

A better breakfast would be a cup of juice or a piece of fresh fruit and a cup of milk with whole-grain cereal. If you are really hungry you can add whole-wheat toast or a bran muffin. This combination of foods will give you a better start for the day than a slice of pizza.

Dear Dr. Cory:
What causes you to throw up?
Why do you sometimes throw up
stuff that tasks terrible?

Kimberly W.
Birmingham, Alabama

Dear Dr Cory,
I've had constipation.
Where does it come from,
and what can I do about it?
Alicia
Michigan

Dear Kimberly:

Vomiting or throwing up is associated with a great many conditions such as respiratory, stomach, or intestinal infections, and allergy to foods, to name a few. These can cause an irritation in the stomach which triggers the vomiting center in the brain to signal the abdominal muscles to contract and thus empty the stomach. This is the body's attempt to eliminate an irritating substance.

If the person vomits several times the bad-tasting liquid from the gallbladder may be present. Normally this bile is stored in the gallbladder, under the liver, and is secreted into the small intestine to aid in digesting food. Vomiting bile means that the irritation to the vomiting center is great. This may mean the person is seriously ill and should see a physician.

Dear Alicia:

Frequent or chronic constipation is typically caused by a lack of bulk or fiber in the diet. Rarely, persisting constipation could be a sign of a more serious problem. If you have constipation often, please check with your doctor. Occasional constipation is not unusual, however, and often it is due to a lack of fiber and fluids in the diet and/or a change in exercise level.

Sometimes all that is needed to avoid this problem is to add more bran, fresh vegetables, fruits, and water to your diet.

Dear Dr. Cory:

I am in fourth grade and I am chubby. How can I lose weight?

Darcey S.
Henderson Michigan

Some good fruits and vegetables that help to alleviate constipation include prunes, figs, dates, raisins, peaches, pears, apricots, beans, raw carrots, celery, cucumbers, lettuce, spinach, and cabbage. Bran is very high in fiber, so it makes a wonderful natural "laxative." It can be used in many foods such as cereals, muffins, oatmeal, casseroles, brown rice, or whole wheat bread.

When you are constipated, avoid constipating foods such as milk, ice cream, cheese, white rice, apple-sauce, bananas, and cooked carrots. Consult your physician before using artificial laxatives or enemas because they can become habit-forming and lead to more problems.

Dear Darcey:

It can be very difficult to lose weight. But you can do it, if you are willing to make some changes in your lifestyle. First of all, you need to change the way you eat. Many people think that they can go on a diet, lose the weight they wanted to lose, and go on eating the way they always did. These are people who gain back the weight they lost because they didn't change any bad eating habits they had. Learn to eat in moderation; this means taking a medium-sized portion of what you eat at mealtime and not going back for seconds. Don't skip meals; that will only make you hungrier later, and you will eat more in the long run. Try to use your willpower to avoid desserts, especially if the dessert is high in calories, such as cake and ice cream. The only in-between-meal snacks you should eat are fruits.

Try to start exercising every day. Find a friend to ride bikes with every day, or take long walks. Soon you will have more energy for other activities. If you follow these few simple rules, you should be able to lose weight. Good luck!

77

Chapter 7

Children Ask Questions About

Tobacco, Drugs, Alcohol

Dear Dr. Cory:
   Why did people bring up drugs and alcohol and cigarettes? How come they invented something that's bad for your health?
                                        Katharine T., age 8

   This is not an easy question to answer, but it is one that sets us thinking.
   Most of the substances adults abuse today were never "invented" for that purpose. They were discovered by accident, as when a primitive man left ripe fruit too long and it fermented and turned into wine. Others were invented by scientists in laboratories, but they were invented for another purpose—to relieve pain, or to cure a disease. Some are useful products used in the wrong way, as when young people "sniff" glue or paint.
   When we talk about the substances abused today we are talking about a wide variety of things. Illegal drugs, of course, but also prescription drugs and some over-the-counter medications. Alcoholic beverages. Tobacco products. Coffee.
   All have one thing in common. They make a difference in the way a person feels. They do this by upsetting the body's chemistry, and overuse of these products will, sooner or later, cause harm to the body. This is the message we need to give our children when they ask questions about drugs.

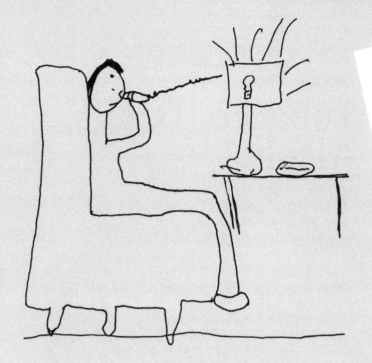

Dear Docter Cory,
My father smokes, I
worry about
him at night. Why do
people smoke? And
how do you help
them stop ~~smoe~~ smoking?
Please help?

P.S. Please don't write
my name write
worried person

Dear Children:

I receive many, many letters like yours. I can't help thinking that if your parents read the letters, if they knew how much you love them and how concerned you are for their health, they would try very hard to stop smoking.

So your first task is to let your parents know how you feel, but in a loving, considerate way. That means you don't nag, or say "yuk" and pretend to throw up every time someone lights a cigarette. Parents don't like to be nagged, any more than children do. The right approach is "I love you very much, and because I love you I want you to take care of your health and live a long time." If you can't easily say this, write it in a letter, and put the letter on the refrigerator door or someplace else where your parent will see it often.

You must remember that what you are asking your parent to do is not a little, easy thing. Stopping smoking is often a very difficult, painful process that goes on for a long time. Because there is

physical and psychological addiction involved, it is not at all like giving up candy or cokes would be for you.

Here are some suggestions:

• A special chewing gum that contains nicotine may help the person give up smoking. The gum provides the same drug that cigarettes give. Later, after a person is used to not smoking, the use of the gum may be decreased or stopped. The gum must be prescribed by a doctor.

• "Stop smoking" classes sponsored by the American Cancer Society or by a local hospital help many people. The people who take part learn more about the problems they are facing, and they help each other through a hard time.

• Support from family and friends can help a great deal. This is where you can do the most good. Ask everyone to be particularly kind to the person who's trying to stop smoking. Try to see that everything goes

80

Dear Dr. Cory,
My DAD smokes
cigars to keep the
Bugs away. Is
hat good for his
ealth?
Shannon S.
East springfielD
PA.

Dear Dr. Cory:
My Daddy smokes a lot. I was
wondering what happens to your
lungs if people like my daddy?
Don't smoke please!
Traci E.
Atkins, Io

smoothly, without fussing or fighting, at home. Suggest that other family members express their appreciation, and that adults refrain from smoking around the person who's trying to stop.

• Suggest that he or she replace smoking with some other activity. This might mean a brisk walk around the block, rather than a mid-morning coffee-and-cigarette break. Learning to knit, or to play solitaire, will give the person something to do with his or her hands while watching TV in the evening. Nibbling on popcorn, celery and carrot sticks, or small sugar-free mints, may help the person who misses having a cigarette in his mouth.

• Encourage the person to try everything and anything—because some methods help one person, other methods help others. Hypnosis, acupuncture, ear piercing, skin patches, taking up a new hobby, wearing a rubber band around the wrist and snapping it when one wants a smoke—these are all ways some people manage to stop smoking. If there is a doctor in your community who specializes in helping people stop smoking, encourage your parent to see that doctor.

• And don't be discouraged if the person fails to stop smoking on the first try. Many people succeed on the second or third try. Don't give up!

• Suggest that the person save all the money not spent on cigarettes, and put it in some special place, and then plan something special to do with that money.

You may be the best person to help your mother or father (or grandma and grandpa) stop smoking. Why? Because they love you, and they want to please you. So let them know how you feel about smoking, but do so in a tactful way.
Good luck!

81

Dear Dr. Cory,
my niebor smoke alot, Will she
get LUng cancer and die.

Kimberly M.
Columbus   ms

Dear Kimberly:

It is quite possible that your neighbor will get lung cancer.

There are many chemicals in cigarette smoke. When a person inhales smoke, these chemicals come in contact with the lung tissue. Some of the chemicals can irritate the lung tissue, and the irritation can lead to lung cancer.

Statistics show lung cancer to be an increasingly common cause of death. In 1984, 85,000 men and 36,000 women died from lung cancer. In 1987, 92,000 men and 44,000 women died from lung cancer. Lung cancer is currently the number one cause of cancer deaths in women in the United States. This shows how serious the problem is.

The people most likely to get lung cancer are those who have smoked many cigarettes per day over a period of years.

Only about 13 percent of lung cancer patients live five or more years once they've been told they have it. That's not very many!

The type of treatment depends on the type of lung cancer and what stage it is in. Doctors can try surgery, radiation therapy, or chemotherapy (using certain chemicals to try to kill the cancer). Often, if the cancer hasn't spread, doctors will try surgery first. However, many people with lung cancer have tumors that have spread into the rest of the body, so radiation therapy and chemotherapy are often used along with surgery.

Dear Dr. Cory,
I had a bus driver who
smoked before he got on the
bus. He doesn't smoke on
the bus but outside of it
would that effect the kids
on the bus?

Erin M.
Armstrong, Iowa

Dear Dr. Cory,
Besides lung cancer, what
can happen to people
who smoke?

Holly B
Dallas, Texas

Dear Erin:

As long as the driver smokes physically away from the bus, not near the open door or windows, it should not harm the children who ride on the bus.

Unfortunately, it does show a bad health example to the children, who watch a respected adult in a very unhealthy, addictive habit.

83

Dear Holly:

Many smokers develop emphysema, which occurs when smoke damages lung tissue. When so much tissue has been destroyed that there is not enough healthy lung tissue left, the person can't get the oxygen his body needs by breathing normally. A victim of emphysema may have to wear an oxygen mask or tube, and wheel a bottle of oxygen with him wherever he goes.

Smoking may also cause Buerger's disease, which affects the tiny blood vessels in the hands and feet and causes them to shut down. When the hands and feet don't get enough blood, sores that can't heal may occur. Eventually the fingers, toes or even a leg may have to be amputated due to gangrene.

Also, smoking is the leading cause of fatal heart attacks.

Doctors believe that smoking may shorten your life by ten years.

Dear Dr. Cory:

I am seven now. When I get older if all my friends smoke except me and they say I am a baby what should I do?

JASON C

Scari ont,

Dear Jason:

Blessings on you, young man! What you are concerned about is called "peer pressure," and it is the chief reason most young people give for starting to smoke.

If you can see the problem so clearly, at the age of seven, I feel sure you will be strong enough to say "No" when the time comes.

It is very important to decide things for yourself, rather than letting other people tell you what to think or do.

Dear Dr. Cory:
Why did they make Cigarettes if there so bad?
Kristy M.
Oceanville. NJ.

Dear Kristy:

Cigarettes and other tobacco products were manufactured and sold for many years before they were known to be harmful. It is only within recent years—within your parents' lifetimes—that we have had certain proof that these products cause illness and death.

Manufacturers go on making cigarettes because they make money this way. Stores go on selling cigarettes for the same reason.

Dear Doctor Cory,

How does smoking form,
Heart ataches and other things?
How can you die from it!

Melissa P
Sharon Massachusetts

Dear Dr. Cory,

What are the effects of
smokeless tobacco? How many
people get killed by it a
year?

Michelle W.
Highbridge, Wisconsin

Dear Melissa:

Smoking affects the heart in different ways. The nicotine in tobacco smoke causes the arteries in the heart to get smaller, so blood can't flow easily to the heart muscle. The arteries can be made temporarily smaller, due to spasm, or permanently smaller, due to build-up in the arteries.

Both can occur at the same time, and you can see how serious this can be. If the flow of blood stops completely a heart attack can occur. Smoking is one of three high-risk factors that cause heart attacks. The other two are high blood pressure and high cholesterol, and smoking can worsen both of these conditions.

Dear Michelle:

Smokeless tobacco (chewing tobacco or snuff) contains the same drug—nicotine—that cigarettes do. The nicotine lifts you up first, then lets you down. The high-low effect on the nervous system sets you up for continued addiction. Research indicates the nicotine in smokeless tobacco is so habit forming it may be more difficult to stop using smokeless tobacco than it is to stop smoking cigarettes.

The American Lung Association's annual report states that 350,000 Americans die annually of smoking-related diseases. The use of smokeless tobacco puts a person at a greater risk for mouth, larynx, throat, and esophagus cancer. It decreases the sense of taste and the ability to smell.

85

Dear Dr. Cory:
  Most of my family smokes cigarettes. My littlest brother is two and he grabs cigarettes and lighters. I grab them from him and smack him. How can my family stop smoking? I've tried everything on commercials and in books and magazine.

Jennifer H.
Melbourne, Florida

Dear Jennifer:

Don't give up! Keep trying. Hypnosis, ear piercing, and nicotine-containing chewing gum are things that work for some people who want to stop smoking.

You mentioned still another danger connected with smoking. That is the fire hazard created by cigarette lighters and young children. Even toddlers can start a fire by rolling a lighter on a rug or carpet.

It is sad to think that smoking might rob your family of health and also of their home, by fire.

Dear Dr. Cory,
Why do people start smoking?

Scott K.
Howell, New Jersey

Dear Scott:

Most people begin smoking for these reasons:
• to gain acceptance by friends
• to express rebelliousness towards adults
• to imitate someone they admire
• out of curiosity

The American Lung Association's latest report shows that the beginning of regular daily smoking is highest among twelve- to fourteen-year-olds, and that among teenagers the daily use of cigarette smoking is greater than the daily use of all other drugs. Hopefully, everyone will soon realize that none of these reasons for smoking is worth the risk of losing his or her life.

Dear Dr. Cory,
My dad has a habbit of smoking.
I Learned that we are not to
smoke. But my dad ~~dos~~ does!
Why do that Yuky thing? Why? Why?

your friend, Tara Jane R

Dr. Cory,
Why do teenagers
smoke pot. Do
they think they
are grown up if
they use it?
Wendy I.
Martinez, CAlif.

Dear Tara:

People start smoking for several reasons but usually continue to smoke because of the addiction to nicotine. This makes it very hard to stop smoking even when a person wants to quit. This is why we encourage people never to start smoking, thus not forming a difficult habit to break.

Dear Wendy:

People who have studied this problem report that most young people who use marijuana do it "to fit in with others." The next most common reason they give is "to feel older."

Many teenagers—and younger children, as well—wish they could be more popular with boys and girls their age. They believe that if they wear the same clothes and hairstyles, go to the same places and do the same things, they will "belong." Unfortunately, when young people see leaders of the group smoke pot, they will want to do this, too.

This is "peer pressure," and it is the number one factor in drug use by young people. When persons, young or old, feel good about themselves and their life goals, the effect of peer pressure is lessened.

87

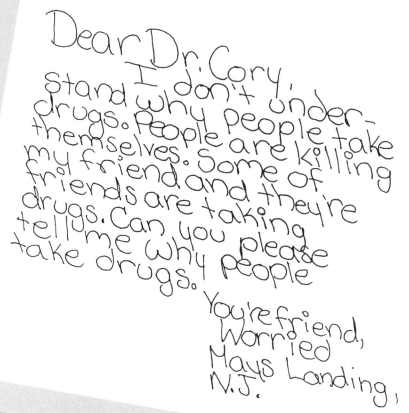

Dear Dr. Cory,
I don't understand why people take drugs. People are killing themselves. Some of my friend and they're friends are taking drugs. Can you please tell me why people take drugs.

You're friend,
Worried
Mays Landing,
N.J.

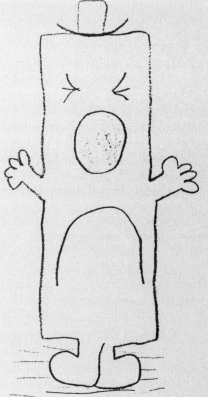

88

Dear "Worried":

Many people take drugs because family members or friends do, because of peer group pressure, to escape problems, to do what they think will give them a thrill, because they want to defy authority figures such as parents or teachers, or because they think it will show that they are mature and tough. However, all they are buying is trouble. And if a person already has problems, eventually drugs and their addictive powers just make their problems worse. If a person were really his own person, he wouldn't have to take drugs (that includes alcohol and smoking) to prove himself to others.

Dear Mary:

All drugs are bad if not used properly. If a drug is used to help treat a particular disease or a specific pain, it can be very helpful and often life-saving. Some people, however, take drugs for other reasons. Some think drugs will help them escape from problems and pressures. Their friends pressure them to take drugs. They think it will give them more confidence and friends, or help their money problems or school grades. These are all wrong reasons to take drugs. Eventually drugs make all of these problems worse.

The drugs that are especially dangerous are those that make your body dependent on them. These drugs include morphine, Demerol, cocaine, and barbiturates. Alcohol; caffeine, which is found in coffee, tea, and many soft drinks; and nicotine, which is found in tobacco, are also addictive drugs. Your body becomes dependent on them mentally and physically. Your body eventually develops a tolerance to these drugs. This means more and more drugs need to be taken to satisfy the dependency the body has developed.

Your best rule is to take medicine only under the direction of your doctor.

Dear Mike:

There are many different drugs that have various effects on different parts of the body. Drugs such as alcohol, marijuana, and cocaine are some of the most often used "street" drugs. Many street drugs at first give the user a pleasurable feeling, but this does not last long. So, in order to continue getting this pleasurable feeling, the user finds that he needs more and more of the drug. This can lead to addiction. Some people can become so strongly addicted to the drug that they may choose the drug over food and water. This can lead to starvation and death.

Drugs can also lower a person's normal social and moral standards. This can cause the person to take risks, such as committing crimes or doing some sort of violence that he would not normally do; not to mention the damaging effect the drug habit can have on the person's family and school responsibilities and relationships.

Young children and teenagers who use drugs also risk slowing their normal growth and development. This can cause lasting physical and mental harm. We only have one body and one mind to last us a lifetime. People who have a healthy respect for themselves and their bodies don't use drugs.

89

. . . About Tobacco, Drugs, Alcohol

Dear DR. Cory:

My mom used to drink 6 or 7 cups of coffee a day. Just recently she stopped. Will this affect her health.

Heather W.
McKeesport, PA.

Dear Heather:

This certainly will affect your mother's health, probably for the better! Drinking too much coffee is bad for you. Coffee has a substance called caffeine in it which is a stimulant. Stimulants can make you jumpy and nervous. They can make your heart beat too fast. So you see, it is good that your mom stopped drinking so much coffee. She will certainly feel better for it.

Dear Dr. Corey
My mom is a helthy person put she always takes pills. She went to the docters about her bad back and they gave her pills. In church she had a tooth ace and she told me took get Three asprin and Back pill. well, She worries me with all the pills She take.

Why does she take all these pills?

from,
Secret girl
Please help me!!!

Dear "Secret Girl:"

You are a good girl to worry about your mother, but please make very sure there is a real problem before you try to do something about it.

Even grownups who are in good general health have aches and pains that require medication. If your mother has had back problems and toothaches at the same time I feel sorry for her, and I'm glad she has something to take for the pain.

Possibly she has some long-term health problem like arthritis for which she must take medicine every day. And perhaps some of the "pills" she takes are just vitamin and mineral supplements.

You do have a right to worry if you know that your mother is seeing different doctors and having prescriptions filled at several different drug stores. If this is true, please tell your father or some other adult you trust and ask them to talk to your mother.

90

Dear Mr. Cory

My Dad is an alcoholic. Sometimes I get scared because my dad gets angry when he drinks. What can I do!

HELP ME! Please

your friend,
C.

Dear C.:

Drinking is your father's problem. You cannot solve it for him. But you may be able to help!

Start by learning something about alcoholism. It is an illness. If your father had cancer you would not hate him for it. So don't let yourself hate him because he drinks! Go on loving him, and let him know it. Include him in family life, and spend time with him when you can.

In most cases it takes outside help, a push of some kind, to get the alcoholic to stop drinking and turn his life around. He can't do it by himself, just by trying harder,

so don't preach or nag him. Be patient and tactful, and do what you can to make family life run smoothly. For example, take younger children away to play when he is angry and shouting.

If possible, get your mother to go with you to a meeting of Al-Anon, an organization for the families of people who drink too much. They may be able to tell you how you can get your father to seek help. Otherwise, discuss the problem with a teacher, minister, or doctor. Don't give up hope! Alcoholism is an illness that can be treated.

91

Chapter 8

Children Ask Questions About

Secret Worries and Fears

Cartoonist Charles Schulz did a great service for parents (and for teachers and doctors, too) when he created the character Linus, the little boy who trails along after the other children, clutching his security blanket.

Linus is the flip side of brash and boisterous childhood. We now know that there is a little bit of Linus in most children. They are worried about babyish habits they can't seem to outgrow. Anxious. Vulnerable. Puzzled by the complexity of family and community life.

This chaper begins with a letter Linus might have written. It goes on to include letters that express a variety of other concerns. Whether or not they voice them, all children have questions about death, divorce, and sexuality. The parent's role is to listen for the unspoken question and to initiate discussion of a topic that may be bothering the child.

Dear Doctor Cory
I have a blanket that I use
at night when I sleep. Like a
sucurity blanket. what should
I do about this?

Jennifer S.

Dear Jennifer:

You don't need to do *anything* about it, so please don't worry. As long as your special blanket helps you feel comfortable and sleepy, hang on to it. Some day you'll just happen to forget about it, and go to sleep without it, and then you'll know you don't need it anymore.

Dear Dr. Cory:
I suck my thumB and I am tring to
stop but I can't

can you geve me good advice

JANA B.
Casa Grande Arizona

94

Dear Jana:

Don't be too discouraged. Yours is a common problem. Many people have had success with a bitter-tasting liquid made especially for this purpose. You can buy it at your local drug store. It is applied to the thumb or finger once in the morning and once at bedtime. Good luck!

How can you loose the habit of biting your nails?

Cassandra B.

Dear Dr Cory
I nibbel my Nails !
I can't stop it
what can Help
me.?

Annie R.

Dear Cassandra and Annie:

Habits are very hard to break, aren't they? One way to break a bad habit is to replace it with a good one. Maybe you bite your nails because you need to be doing something with your hands. Every time you want to bite your nails, find something else to do that will require you to use your hands, such as drawing a picture, painting, putting together a puzzle, sewing; anything you like to do to keep yourself busy is good. Whenever you want to keep from doing something, concentrating on doing something else usually helps.

If this doesn't help, try wearing fingernail polish—maybe a clear color that you can't tell is there once you put it on. Perhaps the taste of the polish will remind you that you don't want to bite your nails. Good luck!

95

Dear Dr. Cory,
My brother has a bedwetting problem, and I've been trying to help him stop. Do yo have any sullutions?

Josh M.
North Ogden, Utah

Dear Josh:

This problem is a common one. Bedwetting occurs in 30 percent of four-year-olds, 10 percent of six-year-olds, 5 percent of ten-year-olds, and about 2 percent of twelve- to fourteen-year-olds. Often one of the parents of a bedwetter was a bedwetter as a child. Boys seem to have this problem more than girls.

Many children with this condition have small or immature bladders (the baglike muscle that holds the urine). Their bladders just won't hold much urine. Sometimes more serious problems can cause bedwetting. A pediatrician can help your brother and parents rule out possibilities.

There are many ways of dealing with bedwetting, including motivational counseling, bladder exercises, medications, and nighttime urine-alarms.

Most children gradually stop bedwetting as they grow older. Meanwhile, have your brother avoid caffeine, which is found in many soft drinks and in chocolate. Caffeine can make you go to the bathroom more often. Have him avoid drinking liquids between dinnertime and bedtime and, of course, go to the bathroom just before going to bed.

Dear Dr. Cory

I am Sherkica and I have this problem that I hope you and solve. It started about two years ago when I heard my mom and dad fussing it was kind of a disagrement. but it ending up turning in to a big fight.
When my parents, do that I think its my fault. My mom says its not my fault. but it doesnt change how I feel. And I don't know what to do about it. Can you help me get reed of this problem

Sincerly Your,
Sherkica

Dear Sherkica:

Your mom is right—it's not your fault, but I can understand that hearing this doesn't make you feel better. I'm sorry that you have to listen to your parents quarreling. They are wrong to talk like this, where you can hear them.

Have you told them both how bad it makes you feel? Have you asked them politely to stop?

You might ask them, when they start to quarrel, if you may leave and go to a friend's house until it's over. You can also try turning up a radio or record player so loud that you can't hear what they say. Some people learn to close their ears to unpleasant sounds, so that they really don't hear what they don't want to hear; perhaps you can learn this trick.

Something you should keep in mind is that grownups don't always mean everything they say. Especially when they get to quarreling, they may say ugly things they know aren't true. So don't believe everything you hear your parents say when they are "fussing."

97

Dear Dr, Cory
I'm having problems with my parents. Ever since they got divorced mom and I have arguments over silly things. How can we prevent them?
Jennifer H.
Miami

Dear Doctor Cory
Why Do peopl have to die when you dont whant them to and what is it like to die?

Yours truly

Betsy

Dear Jennifer:

Divorce is a painful experience for all involved, and often creates a number of confusing feelings. This is natural and expected.

The loss of the family unit causes a grief reaction that is similar to what is experienced when a loved one dies.

It is essential for you to realize that you *did not* and *do not* have a major role in your parents' decision to divorce, and there is little you can do about the way they act towards each other. It is easy to fantasize that if your parents would remarry everything would be great. Often children unconsciously do things to try and make that fantasy come true. In reality, it is your parents who must decide that

issue. The divorce is the result of their decision to live apart. They may decide to date and to find other spouses.

The divorce *does not ever* change the roles your parents have as your mom and dad. Focus on that, and talk to your parents about the relationships of mother to daughter, and father to daughter. Try to understand your mother's situation. She is coping with many changes. She is likely to be irritable, sad, and sleeping poorly. She may have financial problems that result from the divorce.

Make a list of the things you and your mom fight about. Sort them out, and work with your mom to find ways to solve those issues without fighting.

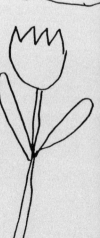

Dear Betsy:

Like most things, life has a beginning and an end. Birth is a natural part of life, and so is death.

None of us knows exactly what death feels like, but some people have had a part of this experience. They are people who became very ill and almost died but then recovered. These people say that what they felt was pleasant rather than frightening. Doctors and nurses who watch over dying people know that the end of life is usually calm and peaceful.

This does not make it easier for us to accept the loss of a family member or close friend. When this happens we may feel anger. What happened seems unfair. We feel sad and lonely. We may feel that we shouldn't play or have fun, ever again. Our life has changed, and it will never be quite the same again.

Some people find it hard to talk about death, or about the person who is gone. This is wrong. We need to talk things out, and to cry, and to share our feelings. Then we can start remembering the good times that we shared with the person who is gone. The person will stay with us, in a special way, as long as we remember.

Dear Doctor Cory,
My Grandmother is really depressed about her Father, he has cancer he is 77 years of age what do you think I should try to cheer them both up

Jenifer D.
Baytown Texas

Dear Jennifer:

The best thing you can do for your grandmother and your great-grandfather is to spend time with them. I hope you live near them, so you can go for short visits every day. They will enjoy hearing what you are learning in school, and about your friends. Maybe they can teach you a card game or a board game. They may enjoy the same after-school TV programs you enjoy, and you can watch together.

Please don't miss the opportunity to learn about their lives when they were your age. This part of your family history will live on with you even after your older relatives have died.

Try to be helpful. Offer to fetch or carry things for them, for example, to take out the garbage or get the mail.

Don't stay too long; your presence may be tiring to elderly or ill people who aren't used to children.

If they don't live near enough that you can visit often, write them letters and send cards. If your mother says it's OK, you might telephone them (long distance calls don't cost much if you call on weekends).

Dear Dr Cory,
I have a problem!
When ever i see a TV
show about sikness
or death for some
reason i think it's
going to happen to
me when i sleep. Please
help me.

Jaimie
Durant, OK

Dear Jaimie:

If you are able to write such a good letter at the age of nine you are probably smart enough to guess what my answer will be.

Don't watch those programs! They are usually on late in the evening, and they're intended for grownups. If your parents insist on watching, you put on your pajamas and go to bed, or go in another room and read a book.

Remind yourself that what you see on TV (except for the news) is made-up stories, and the people are actors just pretending.

It is true that some children get diseases that are unpleasant, and some people die young. But these happenings are very, very rare. They are not things that are likely to happen to you. You are almost certain to live a long and healthy life and die only when you are very old.

A good plan: Make yourself think about pleasant things when you lie in bed. Think about good times you had yesterday, and then start planning pleasant things to do tomorrow, and you will soon fall asleep without being frightened.

100

Dear Dr. Cory:

Can you get
AIDS Drinking
and eating
Behind somebody?

Litina W,
Bascom Florida

Dear Litina:

The good news is that AIDS is not spread by eating or drinking after someone who has the AIDS virus or the disease AIDS. You can't get AIDS by casual contact with someone who has AIDS, as at school.

Dear Doctor cory, What if I'm home all alone and I start to feel drowsey and sick to my stom ach.? should I take any medicine without supour-vision.? Love Rachel

Dear Rachel:

I think you already know what I am going to say: No! Never take any kind of medication on your own. Medicine can do a great deal of good, in the right amounts at the right times, or it can do a great deal of harm if taken improperly, so treat it with respect.

You are right to wonder what you should do if you became ill when alone. This could be a serious problem. Discuss this now, with your mother or father. Make a plan about whom you could telephone, to get help or advice.

In some cities there are special telephone numbers you can call, if you are home alone and frightened or need to talk to an adult. These are sometimes called "Latchkey Kids" programs. Try first to reach your mother, or the person she has told you to call in an emergency, or an adult neighbor that you know you can trust.

Dear Dr. Cory,
I'm 10 years old + I'm starting to show early signs of physical development. My dad thinks I should start wearing a bra, I think I shouldn't
Please explain menstruation to me + when I should wear a bra

BECKY
SCHAUMBURG, IL.

Dear Becky:

Menstruation is a cycle that only occurs in women, and it is a sign that the body is physically matured to the adult state. The puberty changes you have noted will be maintained through your childbearing years.

As the female body matures, it prepares for one of the most important jobs it can do—create and sustain a new life! To do this, the womb or uterus gets ready every month for pregnancy. When pregnancy does not occur, the lining of the uterus is shed. This shedding is normal and natural and healthy, and the small amount of blood and tissue lost is replaced when the body is properly fed and cared for. This monthly cycle of preparation, shedding, and re-preparation continues until pregnancy occurs or until the hormones slow down in later years.

You should wear a bra as your breasts begin to develop, and not wait until the development is complete. The bra is not just for comfort, but for protection and support.

102

Dear Dr. Cory:

Why are boys and girls different?

Debbie

Dear Dr. Cory:

Why does it take two people to make a baby?

Signed,
Kelly

Dear Debbie:

Boys have special body parts that will make it possible for them to be fathers, when they are grown up.

Girls have special body parts, inside their bodies, that will make it possible for them to be mothers when they are grown up.

In the unique plan of creation, all living things have a way to continue the existence of their kind. The need for our human species to recreate and flourish dictates that we should not all be alike. One of the most obvious differences is the difference between male and female. This difference allows for the physical structure and strength of men, and the ability of women to bear children.

Dear Kelly:

I think it's good that it takes both a grownup man and and a grownup woman, together, to make a baby. Have you ever helped to take care of a small baby? If so, you know that it's a lot of work. The baby really needs *two* people to take of it.

Also, children are smarter and stronger and much more interesting because each one has a fresh mix of genes (inherited traits) from the two different parents. The baby receives half its genes from the egg in the mother's body, and half from the sperm from the father's body that fertilizes the egg. As a result, the child will not be exactly like either parent.

103

Index

105